Praise for *LEADING LIGHTLY*

"You've got this! Overwhelmed and exhausted executives now have a roadmap to choose and optimize effectiveness without stress and struggle. *Leading Lightly* teaches you to release inner noise and handle what comes your way with ease and clarity. Jody Michael brilliantly weaves together mental fitness, leadership systems, psychology research, and decades' worth of experience as both a therapist and an executive coach. Using her reliable, data-driven recipe, you can systemically transform leadership for yourself, your team, and your whole organization."

—SUZI POMERANTZ, CEO, Innovative Leadership International; best-selling author; and master executive coach

"Jody Michael sets a high bar for leadership. Her book shows you exactly how to get there, and she makes no apology for dismantling your self-imposed limitations. Get ready to grow."

—MATHEW ELENJICKAL, Founder and CEO, FourKites

"*Leading Lightly* is a truly unique leadership book. Instead of advocating outward actions, it builds your intrinsic strength and psychological resilience, so you thrive in all facets of life and leadership. Jody's tools powerfully effect lasting and transformative change and personal growth, ultimately leading to radical accountability, mental fitness, and happiness."

—OLIVIA NELLIGAN, EVP, Chief Financial Officer, CHS Inc.

"Jody Michael has a secret. And she's sharing it with any leaders brave enough to take lasting action. *Leading Lightly* breaks through a crowded category with a highly actionable playbook designed to put leaders in control of the only thing they actually have control over—themselves. A refreshingly mindful leadership tool in an ever-shifting societal landscape."

—BRENT STEINER, Founder & CEO, Engrain

"Holy Cow! I needed this book so much . . . I devoured it. My first thought was to reach out to every fellow EO member and BrainTrust member—all entrepreneurs and say, 'This book is for *us* . . . you've gotta read it!' But really, this book is for every person in a leadership position. No, wait! It's for every person who wants to be happier and healthier, mentally, emotionally, and spiritually. I'm putting it right up there with *Essentialism* by Greg McKeown as a 'must-read,' 'must-live-by' book."

—SHERRY DEUTSCHMANN, Founder & CEO, BrainTrust

"Leadership is neither a checklist nor formula: it's about your mindset. To increase your impact *and* navigate the toughest situations with clarity and ease, look no further than Jody's definitive book about transformational leadership. She has honed these practical and actionable insights over decades of coaching many of our nation's premier leaders. *Leading Lightly* is a must-read for all leaders, both corporate and civic."

—EDWARD WYNN, Former VP General Counsel and Secretary, Stepan Co.; Executive Chairman, Call One, Inc.

"The best leaders have an ability to both take things seriously *and* hold them lightly. Taking things seriously seems easy enough for most. But to also remain *light*—free of excessive stress, worry, or overwhelm—requires a degree of self-mastery. Jody Michael points the way in this practical and grounded book."

—MICHAEL BUNGAY STANIER, Founder & CEO, Box of Crayons; author of the best-seller, *The Coaching Habit*

"Leading Lightly . . . how profound! When has anyone suggested we adopt a *lightness* in leadership rather than buckling down, being tough, and pushing through? When have we dared to imagine *real* change? I was fortunate to work with Jody Michael as an executive coach. She's brilliant and impactful in her focus on the default perceptual lenses that limit us and repeatedly fail us, our colleagues, and loved ones. Her book, *Leading Lightly*, details her mental fitness approach to leadership, and it's exactly what we all need, now more than ever. It's a method that will serve you well for the rest of your life."

—MARTHA GILMER, CEO, The San Diego Symphony

"I've used Jody's mental fitness and accountability tools in every organization I have led—with powerful results. Learning to lead lightly will change you, not just as a leader, but as an entire person. You'll come to Jody in search of executive coaching—and come out with your whole life transformed."

—MARGARET M. MUELLER, PhD, CEO, Executive Club of Chicago

"Jody Michael is a leadership-effectiveness expert with a proven track record of helping executives maximize their performance. With *Leading Lightly*, she has unlocked the secret to operating at a higher level with noticeable effortlessness on both a professional and personal level. You'll find the practical guidance you need to be your personal best and level up your leadership."

—WANJI WOLCOTT, Chief Legal Officer, Discover

Lower Your Stress,
Think *with* Clarity,
and Lead *with* Ease

LEADING

LIGHTLY

JODY MICHAEL

GREENLEAF
BOOK GROUP PRESS

Published by Greenleaf Book Group Press
Austin, Texas
www.gbgpress.com

Distributed by Greenleaf Book Group

For ordering information or special discounts for bulk purchases, please contact Greenleaf Book Group at PO Box 91869, Austin, TX 78709, 512.891.6100.

Design and composition by Greenleaf Book Group
Cover design by Greenleaf Book Group
Cover image: ©iStockphoto.com/themacx

Publisher's Cataloging-in-Publication data is available.

Print ISBN: 978-1-62634-899-8

eBook ISBN: 978-1-62634-900-1

Part of the Tree Neutral® program, which offsets the number of trees consumed in the production and printing of this book by taking proactive steps, such as planting trees in direct proportion to the number of trees used: www.treeneutral.com

Printed in the United States of America on acid-free paper

21 22 23 24 25 26   10 9 8 7 6 5 4 3 2 1

First Edition

CONTENTS

INTRODUCTION

LEADING LIGHTLY

Sometimes you can't put your finger on exactly what you want.

You're trying to make a decision, or determine a direction, or make some kind of change for the better. You search deep inside yourself for clarity but *what you want* seems elusive, murky, out of reach. However, you're very clear about one thing: You know what you *don't* want. In fact, you might have quite the list: Problems, people, situations—stress of all kinds. Feelings of frustration, anxiety, or sadness. You just don't want any of that anymore.

If you're a leader in today's world, you might have come to a place within yourself where leadership feels like the same difficult grind, day after day, a mix of stress, overload, and exhaustion. You wonder what could change to make it better. Is change even possible? You ask yourself if this is what leadership is and will always be.

I wrote this book because there *is* an alternative. It's called leading lightly.

The funny thing about leading lightly is that in many ways, it's easier to explain what it's *not* than what it is. That's because leading lightly is a particular way of being—a mood, an energy, a frame of mind—that is quite rare in leadership and among people in general. Yet, it is very attainable. And, it is my sincere hope that leading lightly will turn out to be exactly what you want.

So, let's start with what leading lightly is *not*. It is not crashing through your day or just going through the motions in suboptimal states of stress, overload, anxiety, or frustration. It is not struggling through ongoing feelings of heaviness, burden, resignation, or burnout. It is not carrying your stress home with you or taking it out on your innocent significant other. It is not fantasizing about quitting your job and running away forever.

What *does* it mean to lead lightly?

> Leading lightly means that no matter what happens during your day, you have the capacity to approach everything with enduring ease and clarity. It is a state of being that naturally arises when you have learned to let go of your internal noise and emotional clutter.

If you think about light, or lightness, or moving lightly in any context, you can taste a little of the flavor of leading lightly: It's being light on your feet. Light in your mood or lighthearted. Looking from a well-lit perspective. Having a light touch. Turning a lightbulb on. If you're spiritually inclined, then leading lightly is also about the light of a greater consciousness (see sidebar).

In the work setting, leading lightly means that you have the cognitive and emotional (and spiritual) capacity to deal with whatever leadership challenges are brought to you. You're almost effortlessly effective in each moment with your conversations, relationships, decisions, and other actions. You choose your responses with a sense of mindfulness; you're not reactive. You emanate a kind of rare receptivity and have a capacity to metabolize the negative, so that you're not pulled or weighed down.

With each thing that happens, even situations unfamiliar to you, you have an abiding feeling that "you've got this." You're honed and masterful in

LEADING LIGHTLY

A Spiritual Perspective

Most spiritual traditions agree that there is something greater than ourselves at play, something much more expansive and mysterious than the human mind can fathom. "Light" is one of the many names for this, along with consciousness, God, Source, energy, and so on (even "that which cannot be named"). If you are spiritually inclined, then you can understand leading lightly to mean loosening the entrancement of your ego in order to allow more conscious connection or alignment with this greater unseen intelligence or organizing principle.

A spiritual perspective often holds that there is more going on than what we can perceive; that there is something bigger happening in any situation than what our human brain can interpret. The aperture of life is understood to be much wider than the localized impact of any given moment.

From a spiritual lens, leading lightly means getting out of your own way, allowing unfoldment, accepting "what is," trusting in what you can't see, letting go of being right, and receiving the gifts that life itself offers to you. Connecting with universal consciousness in this way, you have access to a deep knowing. You can surf the waves, be in the flow, operate more elegantly, make better decisions, help others get through the storm. In other words, you can lead much more effectively.

moving with what's happening. It's not hard for you to know the right thing to do, because you feel it with an unmistakable clarity inside yourself.

Is this a pipe dream? Pollyanna? Something that only a Zen master could hope to attain? I get it. Being able to lead lightly sure would be great—and so would winning the lottery. If you have your doubts, I understand that. As I said, there aren't many people walking around, at least in a corporate setting, who are leading lightly. But that doesn't mean it can't be done. Most people aren't even aware that it's possible. They believe, on some level, that stress and difficulty are just inevitable. However, if you stay with this book, you'll learn that even your current doubts are *themselves* elements of the noise and clutter that are obscuring what's actually been available to you all along.

Leading lightly comes about from a transformational process that I call MindMastery®. It's a way of discovering, and then shedding, the hidden beliefs, assumptions, and perspectives that create your perceptual lens and underlying operating system. It's not about adding anything new. It's about understanding how your own unconscious thoughts cause you to react in habitual ways that create unnecessary pain, stress, and suffering.

You might ask, Why, if leading lightly is so great, isn't there more of it in the world? Why would something so beneficial be so rare? It's because there is a kind of unconscious wall that every individual must break through, much like the fourth wall in theater. It's as if we are actors in a play on a stage, but we don't know that about ourselves. We don't even imagine that there's any other way to go through life. We react to everything from a kind of limited script and perspective. It's only when someone from the outside—the observers in the audience, so to speak—helps us break that wall and see from a different perspective that we can begin to create something completely different. We may choose to stay on the same stage, perhaps, but we have a different experience altogether.

If I've piqued your curiosity; if leading lightly sounds better to you than your current experience; if you'd rather feel more good than bad in work and life, then please join me on this terrific journey.

1

HOW LEARNING TO LEAD LIGHTLY CAN HELP YOU

This book is going to be all about you. But I need to begin, just for a minute, by talking about me.

The day I lost everything was not a good day.

In the late summer of 1987, I was twenty-nine years old and one of the first female commodities traders on the Chicago Mercantile Exchange. A colleague and I had the audacity to begin building an all-female trading company, Warriors Options Group. We were all in emotionally and financially. Just a few months after we launched, just as we were beginning to trust our growing success, the stock market crashed.

In a matter of hours, we lost everything—more than everything. Not only did we lose all our capital and our company, but we suddenly found ourselves in $50,000 of debt. And, like so many other traders that day, I found myself instantly out of a job. It was not a good day by any typical measure.

At least, that was how it seemed in the moment. I faced a pivotal choice. I could spiral into deep anxiety, despair, shame, and fear of what the future might bring. Or I could *choose* to create something different and alter the course of what would happen next. At this fork in the road of my career and life, I could direct my own experience of these external events. I could be completely devastated—as my business partner and many other traders were. Or, I could be deeply, powerfully energized and focused on creating a different path.

I chose the latter.

In fact, while the day I lost everything was a profound, life-changing experience, it ultimately turned out to be a very good day for me.

AND NOW, BACK TO YOU

You are also, in this exact moment, at your own fork in the road when it comes to your leadership and performance. It's not because you have just received a promotion or prestigious new assignment. It's not that you landed your dream job. Nor is it because a corporate reorganization or acquisition has just pulled the career carpet out from underneath you.

You face this fork simply because you are a leader who has taken responsibility for achieving significant results. Every minute you are not asleep presents you with a decision point: What kind of leader are you going to be *right now*? How are you going to align yourself internally *right now* with what you are trying to achieve? What are you going to choose to create *right now* within yourself and, by extension, within your organization?

Asking these questions should not be a once-a-year performance review exercise. You need to answer these questions every single day. **The strongest driver of results—in your leadership, your team, and your organization— is what you choose to think and feel in each moment.**

There is an ever-present fork in your leadership road.

WHAT WILL YOU CHOOSE?

Your options are deceptively simple.

The first is to allow your brain to run on autopilot as it rapidly executes your well-worn patterns of thought, mood, and behavior. That's the default path that we all take most of the time without any awareness of it. And we don't think of it as a *choice*—if we even think about it at all. That default approach can be fine, or good enough. After all, it has gotten you to this point in your life and career. But it locks you into your current ways of thinking. Not only does that make growth difficult, it virtually guarantees that the things that trigger emotional distress for you today will continue to do so tomorrow and the next day, and the next, and the next, keeping you from being the best you can be.

But the other option—always available to you—is much more revolutionary and transformative. You can *pause*. You can *think*. And then you can *choose* to follow a different and better path, when applicable. Your ability to leverage these thousands of choice points throughout each day—to sustainably create high performance no matter what may be going on—is what I call "mental fitness." Mental fitness increases your capacity, impact, and influence as a leader.

Leadership is about impact and influence. Both grow when you increase your mental fitness.

A FIRST LOOK AT MENTAL FITNESS™

You've likely heard politicians or the news media use the term "mental fitness" to indicate a requisite level of cognitive capability. However, I define it by focusing on *optimized performance*.

Here's my definition:

> Mental fitness™ is your measurable ability to engage constructively in life and work every day, no matter what stressors you encounter. It is your capacity to consistently respond to challenges with optimal performance in the moment and minimal recovery time afterward.

Mental fitness starts with the recognition that the real drivers of your leadership results are the hidden habits of your mind—the powerful, unseen, and entrenched perspectives you hold about yourself, others, and your world. These patterns of thoughts and beliefs (formed by your many experiences in life), whether you are conscious of them or not, drive you to behave in certain habitual ways. And that leads you to produce certain results—for better or for worse.

Mental fitness is most critical and transformative whenever you feel stressed, frustrated, or hindered in any way by your environment or by the people around you. In these situations, you inadvertently become triggered, and you default to behaviors that, to say it kindly, may not be optimal.

What You Need to Know About: Triggers

When you have an intensely negative emotional reaction to something, real or perceived, you have been "emotionally triggered." This means that you are in a strong state of fight or flight. The situation, event, or conversation that you are reacting to is the "trigger."

Triggers can be universal, meaning that just about everyone will have a strong fight-or-flight reaction to the situation in question. For example, if I walk up to you out of the blue and hit you hard across the back with a baseball bat, that act will put you into a state of pain, unless you're Superman. You'll react the same way as everyone else: with a combination of shock, fear, and/or anger. But the triggers I'm talking about are more often unique to the individual. What triggers me might not trigger you, and vice versa.

If I say to one person, "You're fired," they might become frantic, wondering how they are going to pay their bills. Others might feel betrayed: "How can you fire me after all I have done for this organization?" Someone else might feel shame. And the next person might say, "Hallelujah," happy to have been given a push on to bigger and better things.

There is usually a pattern to what will trigger a reaction in any given person. Some people get triggered when they feel that their performance is being criticized. Others get triggered if they feel that they have been misunderstood. For some, it's about perceived encroachment on their turf and possible loss of power. And yet others will get triggered when their integrity is attacked. The nature of a trigger depends on an individual's values, how they see themselves, and their strongest beliefs and biggest fears. Everyone is different.

Throughout, I will explain: a) how to recognize your triggers, and b) how to keep them from getting in your way.

When you're triggered, your leadership performance suffers because your brain is running an internal script rather than clearly assessing and optimally responding to whatever is *actually* happening. It's like endlessly repeating a playlist of your favorite "oldie but goodie" tunes without ever adding new songs to your repertoire. As a result of being stuck in an old loop and interpreting the present through that lens, you are much more likely to make mistakes or poor decisions, damage your relationships, and miss key opportunities.

Many of the pain points that you, your team, and your organization repeatedly have to work through have actually been caused by leaders acting in a triggered state. And when *you* in turn get triggered, you also inadvertently generate pain for others and your organization. It's a vicious cycle.

Mental fitness will help you to avoid much of the pain.

When I talk about eliminating pain points, often people don't believe it's possible. They believe work is supposed to be difficult and sometimes painful. But that isn't really true. The exception to that is someone who is working in the wrong job for their aptitude, and I've seen estimates that put that figure as high as 71 percent of the workforce. Even if it is half that number, that is a depressing statistic. So, yes, if you are in the wrong job, work will be painful.

I personally learned that early on. I remember when I was in college and took a summer job as a daycare assistant. I was thrilled for the opportunity; I loved kids and figured it was going to be great. Who cared that it was minimum wage? I'd get to be with kids all day. But the reality of having five kids tugging on me at once, all needing my attention, and not being able to emotionally attend to each one was overwhelming, heartbreaking, and exhausting. By the end of my first day, I walked up to the owner and said, "You don't need to pay me. Pretend I never took this job, because I can't come back tomorrow."

It was so painful for me that I couldn't emotionally handle it. I was in the wrong job and recognized it right away. Many people either don't recognize they're in the wrong job, or, if they do, they don't have the means to make a change. As a result, people stay in the wrong jobs all the time. And that itself can be painful. While mental fitness can certainly be an asset to help those in the wrong career find a way out, we're going to focus on another kind of pain. It's the pain you experience when you are in the "right" career but have allowed the people and circumstances around you to negatively impact you.

Perhaps it's a toxic environment. Perhaps there's too much to do and not enough time to do it. Perhaps you feel stressed or overwhelmed, and those around you do too, compounding your own sense of pressure. Perhaps you can't get your job done properly because communication is poor or relationships are lacking. Maybe you have to work with one of those notoriously "difficult people" who's a real fly in the ointment. All of these examples are different kinds of pain than the pain of being in the wrong job role. The good news is that you absolutely can do something about it. These are the types of pain we are going to focus on.

With mental fitness, you can keep yourself out of these unproductive emotional states so that you are leading, as much as possible, from a position of optimal performance—so you can *lead lightly*. You do this by very rapidly applying a set of learned skills and choices—the five "muscles" of mental fitness—to change your perceptions and internal reactions:

1. Choose Personal Accountability
2. Choose Helpful Beliefs over Impeding Beliefs
3. Accurately Self-Assess Your Internal State
4. Hold Multiple, Disparate Perspectives
5. Modulate Your Own Physiology

As you apply these five muscles, you intentionally change your perceptions and internal reactions. I will explain each of the five in detail—and how to implement them as we go along. But for now, simply understand that with these choices, you seek to *see yourself and your environment differently*. You break yourself away from those reflexive, automatic reactions that limit potential and possibility in your leadership. With practice, you'll be able to optimize your performance and consistently create new, much better leadership *results.*

A BIG BENEFIT: YOU WILL FEEL LIGHTER

Leaders often feel overwhelmed and weighed down with stress. There is never enough time in the day, the week, the month. The strategy meeting is coming up, quarterly reports are due, and emails don't stop coming in.

My message here is simple: if you develop your five muscles of mental fitness you are going to feel lighter. You will feel more in control. You will lead yourself and others lightly. Many of the negative interactions, feelings, and emotions you are currently experiencing will soften and eventually go away. Rather than getting triggered, you won't take things personally; you'll counter challenges with adaptability and curiosity rather than defensiveness.

A PROVEN APPROACH TO IMPROVEMENT

It's normal to believe that everything around you—circumstances, events, and other people—create the conditions for your leadership performance. For example, you *thrive* in the "right" environment. You're *miserable* in a "toxic" environment, and *your hands are tied* when your direct reports "just don't get it." With mental fitness, you let go of the impeding belief that everything and everyone else is the main problem. You come to your leadership role with a different mindset, deeply understanding that when you want *different* results—for yourself, your team, or your organization—you have to make changes at the root. **That means that change begins with you.**

My proven proprietary method, MindMastery®, will allow you to efficiently and effectively develop a high level of mental fitness. It is a radically different approach to creating and sustaining high leadership performance—as well as personal well-being—especially when the conditions around you are challenging or even painful. Over time, and with practice, this method will lead to you to fundamentally change who you are at your core.

This is not just theory. In all my years working in and with corporate America, I've observed a lot of pain—or, if you prefer, you could say I've seen *an acute level of stress and pressure*. I saw this starting in my days in the trading pits. Granted, I chose to be a trader. In that brutally competitive environment there were only two outcomes played out moment by moment: you won or you lost. But that work environment was akin to a sports competition. Every trader understood this dynamic and accepted that we had voluntarily chosen this pain in return for a chance at a great reward. We had the mentality that we could crush someone in the pit—and then join them ten minutes later for a burger at lunch. No problem.

After the market crash, I took a leadership role on the trading floor with a global financial company. There, I observed that pain or pain points showed up in a very different way. Pain wasn't chosen; it wasn't a game. This pain didn't stop when the bell rang at the end of the day. It deeply hindered business performance, draining and depleting both leaders and employees. Unlike the risk-reward equation in the pits, there was no upside to this type of pain.

I have had an even closer look at the interpersonal and organizational dynamics of these pain points during my past twenty-five-plus years as an executive coach to C-level and senior leaders in fast-moving, highly competitive companies. As a neutral and trusted third party, sworn to confidentiality, I have observed and interacted with top corporate leaders in a very unique, intimate way. These conversations have given me a real sense of the organizational pain and pain points—and their impact—brought about by different types of leaders and their leadership styles.

Here's how these interactions go: I often work with an entire executive team at one time. As I am taken into their confidence as their individual coach, it is not uncommon for several different executives, individually, to tell me about a single, troubling situation in which they were all involved, one that was detrimental to their organization. This puts me in the rare position to hear, for example, three completely different perspectives, told in three vastly different emotional tones, resulting in wildly different versions of the same story that is causing pain for either them, their organization, or both.

Here's a quick example. "Walter" is a C-level executive at a Fortune 100 company who is not sharing intelligence that would allow his people to do their jobs better.

One of Walter's direct reports generally likes him and doesn't think the information secrecy is a big deal. The employee thinks, "Walter's busy. If he thought we needed the information, we'd get it. If we don't, then it means we weren't meant to have it. True, I could do my job better if I had it, but he's the boss." In other words, this subordinate views Walter's actions with positive intent.

The second direct report views the blocking of information as an intentional move by Walter to control power; when Walter knows something no one else does, he is ahead of the game. This direct report thinks, "This is just what some executives do. I will do my best to ferret out the information in other ways. Sure, it wastes my time to have to do that, and it takes me away from the things I should be doing, but there isn't much I can do about the situation."

His third direct report also sees what is going on and feels the hoarding of data is being done with malicious intent. Her take? "Walter is blocking the information to boost his power and to impede the direct reports' ability to do their jobs. Walter is selectively setting up individuals for failure, so he can replace us with people who will be blindly loyal to him."

The only thing these three perspectives have in common is that the executive is hurting the organization. Other than that, they present very different views of a single executive, Walter. When I work with a team like this, I don't question the truthfulness of each version. I understand that each person's story represents their particular perception and perspective. But I do look at how each person *created* their perspective. (We'll talk about this in depth when we explore perceptual lenses in the next chapter.) And, of course, I probe further to find out what is really going on. I have a strong sense of what works in the real world and what doesn't. And I don't believe you're going to find theoretical musings here that will waste your time.

A LACK OF MENTAL FITNESS

Leadership pain points drastically hinder company performance. That is the unarguable conclusion I have come to after decades of working with executives. The problem is far more prevalent and impactful than shareholders and investors could ever possibly imagine. Sometimes the order of magnitude is literally billions of dollars, played out over a period of several years.

It is easy to see why the cost is so high when you see the kinds of situations my clients typically face:

- Machiavellian power moves, like Walter's, driven by a leader's distrust or self-interest rather than what's in the best interest of the organization
- Costly bottlenecks when leaders, stuck in their own discomfort, drag their feet on making decisions; also known as analysis paralysis, risk avoidance, or passive-aggressive resistance
- Disengagement of direct reports (or the workforce at large), driven by leaders who berate and reprimand, emphasizing what's wrong over what's right, and/or who must always show up as the smartest person in the room
- Low morale and impaired productivity arising from a pervasive organizational watch-your-back culture of defensiveness and blame
- High turnover and loss of talent and human capital when the organization's best achievers choose to opt out of the negative relationships and cultures driven by a high-level leader's destructive values and behaviors

Far too much leadership energy gets wasted as people strategize to work around these problems. This interpersonal and institutional friction creates tremendous misalignment and inefficiencies, hindering organizations from moving forward.

The problems I am describing are not the normal and healthy disagreement that often occurs in discussions about corporate strategy and the like. It is about leaders who are rigid, controlling, or fearful. Leaders who are unaware, embody low emotional intelligence, and lack the capacity to see beyond their own self-interests. These damaging leaders are both unaware of what they are doing and are unable to stop it.

If one to three out of twenty top leaders in an organization (and that's a typical number, from what I've observed) exhibit the kinds of detrimental behaviors listed above, then that entire group of twenty wastes time and energy dealing with the resulting pain. This is energy that both individuals and organizations cannot afford to waste; it's needed for building and driving the enterprise. And the waste we are talking about is not just at the top—the inefficiency, damage, and disengagement ripple out in all directions, across and down all functions of the organization.

Nor do the pain points always end in the workplace. Leaders and employees take home their frustration, anger, or resignation. Drained and depleted, they are not able to be present with those they love. They may be physically sitting in the same room, but they are not really "with" their family. The pain they are in follows them around and affects everyone they come in contact with.

YOU ARE GOOD. MENTAL FITNESS CAN MAKE YOU GREAT!

It is no accident that you have come to hold the leadership role that you do and that you have chosen to read *this* particular book at *this* particular point in your career. Everything you have done to date has brought you to this moment. The decision you made to engage with the ideas and methods we will be discussing shows you have within you the capacity to lead and live in a whole new way. As you do, you will inevitably impact, in a positive way, the many other people who are in your extended sphere of leadership influence.

My executive coaching clients have shown, again and again, that developing mental fitness measurably reduces individual and organizational pain points and optimizes performance. It also becomes much easier to create alignment and move faster. The beneficial results of all this are seen in financial metrics such as reduced or avoided operational expenses, reduced or avoided risk exposure, increased sales, and the expansion of the business through innovation in products and services.

When you became a leader in your organization, you signed up for a big responsibility and you need to perform at a high level—consistently and reliably. And you want to feel good, vital, and alive along the way. This book will provide you with a pragmatic process for developing your mental fitness in order to optimize and sustain high work performance and personal well-being. This book will lighten your load and lift the current weight you carry on your shoulders by putting you in control of your experience.

As a result of what you learn here, you'll meet your leadership responsibilities and move your organization forward in a way that *also* energizes and enlivens you. In fact, with well-developed mental fitness, you will ultimately find yourself creating results in both work and life that are probably far beyond your current expectations. You will feel different. You will feel lighter. And, you and others around you will notice and feel it too.

Third-party research conducted by the strategic research and consulting firm, Shapiro+Raj, has shown that many of my clients who have become proficient in MindMastery

- Have more energy
- Experience less stress
- Stop taking things personally
- Build emotional intelligence
- Feel more in control
- Respond to situations with agility and resilience
- Achieve results quicker and with greater ease
- Build deeper trust and stronger interpersonal relationships
- Build mindfulness and break through self-imposed limitations

By applying the Five Muscles of Mental Fitness™, you can measurably transform results for you, your team, and your organization—even under stressful conditions.

For some people, increasing their mental fitness is about being the best leader they can be. For others, it is about maximizing organizational performance. And for others still, it is more akin to a personal spiritual path. The commonality in those three objectives is *transformation*.

As you look at the world in a new way you will stop creating pain; you will start creating performance. You'll breathe new life into your leadership, inspire others, and create the best possible outcomes in a world that very much needs you to be your best possible self. Let's get that transformation underway.

Key Points

- **Pain** in the workplace is not mandatory. You can stop the cycle.
- **The strongest driver** of results—in your leadership, your team, and your organization—**is what you choose** to think and feel in each moment.
- **Mental fitness** measurably reduces individual and organizational pain points and **optimizes performance**. It becomes much easier to create alignment and move faster.
- **Leadership is about impact and influence**. Increasing your mental fitness will improve both.

2

CREATING MENTAL FITNESS™

Q: Why must I be mentally fit in order to lead lightly?

A: If you are not mentally fit, you are handicapping yourself.

If you are often or easily triggered or threatened, or lack self-awareness, you are not using your full capacity. You're not necessarily seeing the impact of what you're saying and doing. You don't necessarily have a wide enough aperture to be able to make the best decisions. As a result, you might not be open to listening to or hearing other people's opinions. All of these traits are going to diminish your capacity to drive results and be the leader who's effective in aligning everyone and is the calm in a storm when people get anxious or worried.

When you are reactive, or when you are not leading lightly, you're not very skilled at situational leadership. You're not very nuanced and effective in those moments that you need to be. You have to have a level of mental fitness to be able to lead lightly.

But having mental fitness is equally powerful in the opposite way. When you are mentally fit enough to lead lightly, you will have more energy because you're not going to be physiologically or emotionally challenged for the vast majority of the day. You will have more capacity to take on new initiatives and to delegate most effectively. You'll be able to be far more strategic.

If you want to create mental fitness, you need to know what it is and what it looks like. And the easiest way to picture it is to draw an analogy to physical fitness—because the two are similar in both their definitions and how we develop and measure them.

So, what does physical fitness mean to you? When I ask my clients, they typically say:

- "I can go for a run (or swim or hike or bike ride) and my body can keep up with the demands."
- "I have more than enough energy to get through the day, both at work and at home."
- "I have the ability to keep taking on more. I become capable of handling more weight, distance, or speed."

Those are all examples of the outcomes of being physically fit. You can think of physical fitness as your ability to execute daily activities with optimal performance. Notice this is not just slogging through your daily activities, or executing them in any which way. It is carrying them out with *optimal performance.* That last part is key.

Mental fitness comprises both choices and skills, and it is measurable.

When we lack physical fitness—when we are out of shape—then physical activity can feel like a struggle. There is a difference between what we desire to do and are able to do. At first it might not be noticeable, but, as it grows wider and wider, that gap becomes a real impediment to us enjoying life. And when it gets bad enough to affect our daily life we typically start thinking about how to change our diet and lifestyle.

I want you to think about mental fitness in a similar way: executing your daily activities with optimal performance. In this case, your daily activities (both at work and at home) are not those that are physical, they are your mental exertions. Every day, all day long, you solve problems, make decisions, navigate relationships, hold crucial conversations, make plans, take actions, and drive results. In this context, optimal performance means your mind is clear, sharp, and focused. You're using all of your brain for the issue at hand. You're quick, agile, and strong.

When mental fitness is lacking, it is easy to feel overwhelmed and chronically stressed by the demands of the day. You are anxious, worried, or doubtful that you are going to be able to carry out your tasks and responsibilities to your high standards. In these situations, we really don't think about, or strive for, optimal performance. We are just trying to make it through the day.

Now, this may not apply to you, especially if you feel you are totally on your game. (You probably have a history of achievements to prove it, too.) Even still, I assure you that you have much to gain from increasing your mental fitness. Even the most accomplished executives I've worked with have blind spots that are holding them back in some way.

For example, you may be:

- Blind to how you are perceived
- Blind to your perspectives and cognitive biases
- Blind to your deeply reactive, automatic responses
- Blind to your well-honed defense systems

Most of us never really go "under the hood" to understand the repetitive strategies we employ on a daily basis to avoid pain: The pain of feeling inadequate. The pain of being wrong. The pain of future loss. The pain of humiliation. The pain of shame. The pain of believing I'm not smart enough. Most of us remain blind, or unconscious if you will, throughout our life. We're unaware of what's actually driving our behavior (or lack of behavior), the decisions we make, and the ones we avoid. Many of us actually believe these limiting behaviors are simply "who I am." It becomes a self-defeating declaration that drives the continued less-than-optimal behavior, setting the foundation for a distorted perspective that doesn't allow for change.

The takeaway? Even if you are performing at a high level now, what will take your performance to the next level is your capacity to see yourself, in the moment, in the now, and be able to manage those moments that sabotage your performance, your decision-making capacity, and your capacity to communicate effectively.

In other words, you need improved mental fitness.

Mental fitness is best achieved by making a specific set of choices and developing core skills that transform your fundamental approach to work and life from stress-driven reactivity to powerful, growth-driven engagement.

WHAT IS MENTAL FITNESS?

Mental fitness is your measurable ability to engage constructively and positively in life and work every day, no matter what stressors you encounter. If you are mentally fit, you consistently respond to challenges with optimal performance in the moment and minimal recovery time afterward. Let's unpack that definition.

Engaging constructively and positively means you are open, curious, and engaged. You are optimistic, creative, and relational. With mental fitness, you are engaging positively in both life and work. Mental fitness doesn't occur just sometimes or only in certain contexts. When you are truly mentally fit, it is evident across the full spectrum of your daily activities—from the time you wake up until the time you fall asleep.

Anabolic Mental Fitness

In our metabolic system, the anabolic process rebuilds muscle through hormones that "build up" and rejuvenate your system, especially repairing the wear-and-tear that occurs during destructive catabolic processes that break down materials for energy. In *Leading Lightly* and in MindMastery coaching, we use this same idea to describe a person's mood state and energy presentation, following the model first described in Bruce D. Schneider's book, *Energy*

Leadership. Anabolic refers to the individual maintaining a highly sustainable state of flow, focus, and engagement. Their overall state has beneficial impacts for both them and the people around them.

This is in stark contrast to what is more typical: a chronic state of distress, much like the catabolic state, where you are defensive, reactive, and fearful and your body is constantly manufacturing stress hormones like adrenaline or cortisol.

Now you might ask about a middle ground. What if I am able to effectively deal with some stressors better than others, or some of the time but not always, based on things I've learned in the past? Here's my answer: if the way you handle challenges depends upon a confluence of just the right context, people, and/or circumstances, that is not mental fitness, it's likely the application of techniques or tactics. Techniques and tactics are only good so long as they happen to exactly fit a situation; they don't provide the fluency that enables you to meet *any* life or work challenge or stressors that come your way.

What You Need to Know About: Stressors

The second part of the mental fitness definition is engaging positively *every day, no matter what stressors you encounter.* Think about when you say you feel "stressed," whether at work and at home. Then think about what you would say caused that stress. Whatever those causes are—whatever you believe creates stress for you—is a stressor.

Stressors can be external or internal.

- **External stressors:** many competing demands, interactions with difficult people, lack of organizational clarity, lack of resources, parenting, relationship issues, household management, and demanding financial obligations
- **Internal stressors:** a critical inner voice; low self-esteem, feelings of inadequacy or low self-worth, low risk tolerance, distrust, or lack of safety

Mental fitness does not eliminate all the challenges in life—unfortunately, nothing can do that—but mental fitness will allow you to better deal with those challenges. And, in this case, "better" means faster, more efficiently, with far less angst, and with quicker recovery afterward. All of us will experience pain in life. Mental fitness is about both managing that pain and understanding that there are times when you are actually the one creating that pain unnecessarily.

When you are mentally fit, there is a consonance: you feel good inside (mentally and emotionally); your physiology is calm (no stress); *and*—very important—the people around you also observe and would agree that you are present, at ease, listening, open, and authentic. Without that consonance, you have something that may look like mental fitness, but is far from it.

FAUX MENTAL FITNESS: LOOKALIKES

When how you feel inside is a stark contrast to how others experience you, then you're lacking mental fitness.

For example, you may feel calm, cool, and collected, but you create a stressful environment for others that interact with you. Or, your outward appearances indicate that you are measured and in control, yet your colleagues would say that is because you are avoiding crucial decisions; you are not engaging in any difficult actions. Your feeling of calm is coming about because you are not engaging in potentially difficult conversations. You're avoiding.

Alternatively, if you feel stressed out or unhappy inside, but no one else is aware of it because you act like everything is just fine, you're lacking mental fitness.

When mental fitness is truly present, everyone experiences it.

Mental fitness is about the ability to respond to challenges effectively. *Responding* is very different from *reacting*. When you respond, you consciously evaluate your situation, choose an intentional, specific action (including none, if that's the most appropriate response), and then act accordingly. Everyone can do this sometimes, but with mental fitness you can do this repeatedly, time after time, no matter how triggering or stressful the circumstances.

THE BEST YOU CAN BE

Now let's discuss the final part of our definition of mental fitness: you **consistently respond to challenges with optimal performance in the moment and minimal recovery time afterward**. It's not enough for us to simply respond to challenges; we need to do so with optimal performance in the moment. That means your thought patterns and moods do not interfere with your ability to capitalize on your talent and cognitive ability. It also means you are not in a threatened or triggered state in which you lose capacity. And you are not physiologically tense.

For example: You're a pro basketball star, and you're at the free throw line for the winning shot in the championship game. Tens of millions of people are watching. Are you going to miss the shot because of the pressure of the moment? Because your muscles are contracting and you are second-guessing yourself, wondering if the free throw is going to go in?

Or, are you going to bring your very best—physiologically, psychologically, emotionally—to that moment, optimizing your performance?

Mental fitness is the latter, of course.

Now, you could still miss the shot for other reasons, but at least it would not be because you were working against yourself in that critical moment of performance. This ability to consistently excel under pressure, to exhibit mental fitness, is what separates the clutch performers, the superstars such as LeBron James in basketball and Tom Brady in football, from everyone else.

Every day there are free throw moments. Whether it's conscious to us or not, there is an underlying sense that stakes are very high, and we feel pressure, tension, or stress. These are the moments that call for us to be at our mental fittest: to perform, optimally, under pressure. The better we can perform in these moments, the more our personal brand grows and our potential is noticed by others.

HOW TO MEASURE MENTAL FITNESS

Mental fitness, like physical fitness, is measurable. There is no need to guess or approximate. We can use quantitative terms to understand where we're starting from, how much progress we've made, and where we can still improve. We can do all those things using what I call the Mental Fitness Index™.

Your Mental Fitness Index is a measure of your ability to use all Five Muscles of Mental Fitness™ together in your moments of greatest pressure. The index is a measure of your speed and agility in shifting out of that emotionally triggered state. After all, the whole reason for developing our mental fitness is to perform optimally no matter what is thrown at us. So, we want to measure it when the pressure is greatest.

MENTAL FITNESS INDEX

I have developed a robust, reliable assessment that I use with my workshop and coaching clients both at the beginning and end of our work together. With approximately eighty items, this instrument identifies areas for development in each of the five individual muscles of mental fitness, as well as indicates the overall success in using the muscles all together to rapidly and consistently shift out of a triggered state. As a posttest, it measures the progress that has occurred through all the work the client has done to change their brain.

There are two metrics in the Mental Fitness Index, both based on measures of time. The first part is **speed**: How quickly can you minimize reactivity and shift out of your triggered state? It's not uncommon for people to ruminate, fret, and worry about something for days or even weeks, maintaining an ongoing catabolic (negative) state.

However, as you develop mental fitness, you'll need less and less time to make the shift. The ultimate goal is to shift in just seconds. And it is possible! But the important point to remember is that the change is gradual. With practice, you will get better at it over time. Eventually, you'll need less and less time to make the shift to the positive, proceeding productively.

The second part of the Mental Fitness Index is **sustainability**. While any quick and agile shift is an important success to be celebrated, we can't say that mental fitness is truly present until we see that shift reliably happen again and again, day after day, across a variety of challenges—no matter what life throws at you.

As we said earlier, it is certainly possible for any individual to handle a particular challenge well, or even optimally. That could be a moment of peak performance, or a coincidental alignment of the challenge with their particular strengths. But just because you can do it once does not mean you are mentally fit.

In order to distinguish between true mental fitness and the occasional effective performance, we need to look at the repeatability or consistency of how you handle challenge after diverse challenge over a period of time (months), in your normal everyday environment.

Put another way, shifting out of an emotionally triggered state is *the* measure of mental fitness. It is in-the-moment use of all the mental fitness muscles, the real-time application of the personal choices (accountability, helpful beliefs), plus skills (accurately self-assessing your internal state, holding multiple and disparate perspectives, modulating your physiology).

So, when it comes to measuring your mental fitness, the key variables are:

- You can shift out of your triggered state quickly; and
- You can do it over and over again, sustainably.

MENTAL FITNESS QUIZ

While the Mental Fitness Index is the very best way to reliably assess your own mental fitness in all its dimensions, this quick quiz will provide a general sense of your current level of mental fitness development. As you recall, mental fitness is not only the ability to rapidly shift out of a triggered state, but to do so permanently no matter what. This means you can consistently do so in almost any scenario at work, home, or any other context.

Caveat: This quick self-test will not be reliable if you have minimal self-awareness, if you tend to avoid or dismiss uncomfortable feelings, or have a tendency to check out or numb yourself when things start to feel difficult.

Instructions

Read and determine which *one statement* below is most like you, most of the time. Be honest with yourself!

When I get triggered—I get anxious, defensive, angry, upset, ruminating, checked out, or shut down—in a particular kind of situation or scenario . . .

A. I stay triggered. Whatever is bothering me lingers or stays with me, or at some point I just move on to something else, or I purposely distract myself out of it.

B. I can get myself out of the triggered reaction, but that sense of peace or relief doesn't last very long. The thoughts and feelings come right back a few minutes later, and I'm triggered almost as much as I was before.

C. I can get myself out of the triggered reaction within a few minutes. Then I have some peaceful time, maybe an hour or so. But the thoughts and feelings I had around that scenario do come back, and I get upset or shut down again.

D. Not only can I get myself out of the triggered reaction within a few minutes, but it's pretty much gone for good because I have changed the way I am viewing the situation. Later on, I might have some fleeting trigger-type thoughts about the situation, but there's no emotional charge. I don't grab onto the thoughts and go down the rabbit hole with them. They just kind of pass through my mind without sticking.

E. I get myself out of the triggered reaction within minutes, and it's a permanent shift. No thoughts of that situation return. If that scenario happens again at another time, I again quickly and permanently get out of the trigger each time.

F. I no longer even get triggered at all in that type of scenario whenever or wherever it occurs. It's a nonevent.

G. *None of the above seem to apply to me.* Either I'm not sure how I handle triggers, or I don't think I really get triggered, or I just don't really let things bother me.

What Does Your Answer Mean?

If your answer is A, B, C, or G

Your level of mental fitness matches that of most people. You're at the starting line—and that's just fine! By reading this book, you're definitely putting yourself in the right place—and you're really going to enjoy the benefits that will come as you develop your five muscles of mental fitness.

Was *G* your answer? You may be wondering why I say you're at the starting line. It's likely that you are dealing with triggers using a strategy of avoidance, not mental fitness. People with mental fitness have a high level of self-awareness and they know *exactly* how what they are doing in order to manage themselves and their moods. It doesn't just happen without them knowing how.

If your answer is D

It's clear that you've already done some work to increase your mental fitness, using one methodology or another. You've got at least a moderate level of mental fitness. This book will help you get to the next level. Reread items *E* and *F* in the quiz, because those represent the next level for your growth.

Know that your ultimate goal is to be able to consistently shift in this way across all the different *domains of your life*—in work or professional scenarios, home scenarios, and other personal-life scenarios. At that point, you'll have achieved a high level of mental fitness.

If your answer is E or F

You've got a solid level of mental fitness. Now ask yourself: Can you consistently shift in this way across all the different *domains of your life?*

If your ability to make these shifts is still dependent on the external context (for example, you do it at work but not at home, or vice versa; or you can do it with some triggers but not the majority), then your next step is to keep working to expand your consistency. This book will help you do that.

If you can make these shifts no matter what the context—no matter who the players are, or what and where the trigger occurs—then congratulations! You have a high level of mental fitness that will serve you well throughout your life. You probably don't need this book for yourself, but you might use it to help others.

Initially, you have to apply the MindMastery process all the time. You will be triggered often and repeatedly. But, in response, you exercise your choices and skills. You build your muscles. You still have ups and downs, because you're learning, you're developing, you're changing how you think. However, over time, you get faster, quicker, more agile. Eventually, there is less need for you to make these shifts, because all these choices and skills become integrated into who you are. They become the new automatic way of being, and so many potential points of triggering are avoided altogether.

When triggers do happen—and they will, because you are human— you'll have the capacity to quickly get out of it without any negative methods such as drugs, disassociation, rationalization, etc. Real mental fitness is walking lightly on the earth.

CAN EVERYONE DEVELOP MENTAL FITNESS?

After working with thousands of clients in my executive coaching and psychotherapy practice, I have found that almost everyone has the potential to significantly improve their level of mental fitness and greatly improve their quality of life as a result.

A few notable exceptions are individuals with certain mental illness diagnoses. People with extreme narcissistic tendencies will have a difficult time as well. (See sidebars.)

Those who struggle with anxiety and depression, however, who may have been in therapy for years and feel they have stagnated, have found my method for developing mental fitness extremely helpful in making real breakthroughs. Some have even successfully tapered off their psychotropic drugs (with the guidance of a medical professional) and eventually have gotten off them completely as they have rebuilt targeted neurosynapses in their brain using this adapted CBT MindMastery methodology. But let's focus on the wide range of people who do not have intractable or lifelong mental illnesses.

Mental Illness and the MindMastery® Process

For a relatively small group of people, our mental fitness process will not yield the same results. What I have experienced in my clinical and coaching practice is that some people who are likely to face limitations when it comes to mental fitness are those with severe, intractable mental illnesses such as schizophrenia, borderline personality disorder, bipolar I, antisocial personality disorder (which can include both sociopaths and psychopaths), and other severe personality disorders.

Dealing with Narcissistic Leaders

Narcissism is a topic we need to touch on because there are a fair amount of executives who have a narcissistic personality disorder or who score quite high on the spectrum.

Why are narcissists so prevalent in leadership positions? Well, they are, as Michael Maccoby, a psychoanalyst, put it in a classic Harvard Business Review article twenty years ago, "skilled orators and creative strategists. Narcissists have vision and a great ability to attract and inspire followers. They also pose the critical questions."

But those benefits come with an extremely high cost. Countless leadership pain points are created by narcissistic leaders. The problem is narcissists don't see the damage they do; they are blind to all the pain they create in the organization. They don't take other people's perspectives and views into account, and they are not working for the collective good of the team or the organization. They are out for self-glory and are extremely sensitive to criticism or slights, which "feel to them like knives threatening their self-image and their confidence in their visions," writes Maccoby.

continued

He offers three very useful rules for working with narcissistic leaders that I wholeheartedly endorse.

1. Always empathize with the leader's feeling, but don't expect any empathy back. Narcissists are not empathetic.
2. If you believe the leader is wrong about something, show them how a different approach would be in their best interest.
3. Hone your time-management skills. "Narcissistic leaders often give subordinates many more orders than they can possibly execute. Ignore the requests that don't make sense. The leader will likely forget about them anyway."

As you think back to the analogy of physical fitness, it is obvious that some people seem to get fit with less effort than others. There are variations in body type and genetics. There are lifestyle variations that do, or do not, support the effort—for example, nutrition, vitamins and supplements, hydration, sleep quality, and social support. And there are personal differences, such as mindset and commitment. The same is true for mental fitness. The potential to achieve it is there for everyone, but there will be variations in the amount of effort and time required for different people to develop it.

I hesitate to detail the reasons why because the last thing I want you to do is grab onto any one of them as an excuse for why you personally are going to be limited in what you can achieve. But the fact is, there are going to be both genetic and environmental influences that may affect where anyone is starting from and how much effort and time they might need for development.

For example, some people are naturally hardwired to be more reactive (or easily triggered) than others. Conversely, some have engaged in meditation or other practices that have already honed some of the components of mental fitness. I urge you not to dwell on any normal differences such as these, or use them to make unhelpful assumptions in either direction—either that you won't really be able to develop mental fitness, or that you are already as mentally fit as you are ever going to be.

THE MUSCLES OF MENTAL FITNESS: A BRIEF INTRO

When we want to become more physically fit, we work our bodies. Sometimes we concentrate on specific muscles—such as our biceps or quads—and strengthen them by boosting the number of reps with gradually increasing weights. Other times we work our whole body at one time, such as when we run, swim, kickbox, or use an elliptical machine.

In mental fitness, we can also work both individual "muscles," as well as the "whole system." Let's do a quick introduction to the five muscles of mental fitness that we will be talking about in detail in the chapters ahead.

Two of the five, Accountability and Helpful Beliefs, are personal choices that you make. The other three, Self-Assess, Hold Multiple Perspectives, and Calm Your Physiology, are skills that you build. All five can and should be developed individually. But you can and should also practice and use all of them together, in a holistic or systemic way, in moments of greatest distress or triggers, that is, when you are in a catabolic state.

You may be thinking that making a choice—the first two muscles we are going to talk about—is not really a muscle in the same way that developing a skill is like a muscle. But isn't it? Think about any choice that you find hard to make but face regularly, again and again. For example, it could be the choice to eat that high caloric snack right now (or not); to go to the gym right now (or not); to speak your mind to your boss right now (or not).

Any change that you want to make at your workplace or in your personal life will require you in some way to face real-time choices—and to change your typical choice to something different. Just like developing a muscle, making that different choice may feel harder in the beginning, or it may be challenging to keep doing so consistently. But eventually, the more you continue to consistently *exercise* your desired choice, the easier it gets.

Now, let's take a brief look at the muscles themselves. (They each will be getting a full chapter later on.)

Although you can't see the "muscle" that works to make a particular choice, it is indeed there and it can indeed be strengthened with intention and practice.

MUSCLE 1: ACCOUNTABILITY

You'd be surprised how many people incorrectly think they have already mastered this one, and believe they can simply move on to muscle number two. Invariably, they are wrong. When I say you need to choose personal accountability, I'm not talking about everyday actions like showing up for work on time or taking your son to baseball practice, although that is certainly part of it. I'm talking about a radical level of accountability. You stop blaming other people and/or circumstances for how you feel or what has happened to you.

You own *all* your thoughts. You own *all* your mood states. You own *all* your behaviors (including avoidance or non-behavior). And, you fully own your part in your results, even while recognizing other potential contributions to what has unfolded. In other words, with mental fitness, you own exactly what's yours and you hold others to own what's theirs.

What You Need to Know About: Mood States

For a moment, imagine yourself in a "good mood," a recent time when you were feeling pretty okay about your day. Now, imagine yourself in a "bad mood." Think of having an off day rather than a flash of extreme anger. When you experience a general feeling for some time (more than a quick burst), this is what I call your mood state.

It includes your thoughts, feelings (the mood itself), energy level, and related physical sensations. It's like when we say someone has a "dark cloud hanging over their head," or "they're really on fire today," or "something's really eating at them."

Psychology research and literature make clear distinctions between moods, feelings, and emotions. But to develop your mental fitness, we don't need that level of precision. For our purposes, we will interchangeably use the terms mood, mood state, feelings, and emotions.

MUSCLE 2: HELPFUL BELIEFS

Most of us think that our beliefs are truth. But if you give that idea a moment's thought, you'll realize that isn't the case. You'll understand that "my beliefs" are "the world according to me," and your beliefs are "the world according to you." Beliefs are a core part of our perceptual lens and thus very powerful in shaping our everyday experiences. But they are not facts.

Beliefs are actually a set of assumptions, and as such we can experiment with them: We can probe them, challenge them, and try on new ones. In fact, beliefs are actually a *choice*. We just don't think of it that way, because most of our beliefs were indoctrinated into us as we grew up, influenced by the people, cultures, and institutions around us, as well as what we experienced. We took on our beliefs without ever realizing it.

Perceptual Lenses

There are all kinds of perceptual lenses, and every person uses different lenses at different times. That said, each of us tends to use, and overuse, our own few personal favorites. For example, when someone has a **competitive lens**, they will relate to almost any situation as though it is a competition, whether or not any such competition exists. Someone with a **binary lens**, something I see a lot in my coaching, will relate to most situations as if there is only one right answer, and everything and everyone else is wrong. There is no gray area, middle ground, or flexibility.

Working with lenses is really about two things:

1. Expanding our awareness of lenses we don't currently use, and
2. Using all of our lenses selectively as may be appropriate to the context.

Typically, we each have a few favorites that we apply no matter what the context. Occasionally, just by chance, we are applying the most appropriate lens. But because we are using these few lenses by default, a lot of the time it is not appropriate to the context. We are both unaware of that and unable to change because we lack exposure to, or awareness of, alternatives. We need to expand past our tired old playlist. Consider how each of the following additional common perceptual lenses brings a unique interpretation to any situation. Try to also think about people you know who embody these lenses.

This discussion has two parts: generally helpful lenses, and those that are impeding when overused.

Generally helpful lenses:

- **Collaborative lens.** The I-win-when-you-win-approach. This is an empathy-driven "we" focus. Maybe everyone doesn't get everything they want, but everyone is walking away feeling heard and included.

- **Optimistic lens.** "Everything always works out for the best, even if it doesn't seem so in the moment." Just about everyone can recall a time when something they thought was terrible ultimately turned out to be a very good turn of events. For example, someone is suddenly dumped by their romantic partner, but then finds the true love of their life a year later. This lens can be powerful and effective. Research shows that with this lens, you are going to live longer, be happier, and show more resilience. Could it be dangerous? Sure, if you are a CEO living in La-La Land, you may ignore the data that clearly shows you need to make drastic changes and say, "Oh, it will all work out." You need to know when to move, and when to react.

- **Create possibility lens.** This is a designer lens! It temporarily sets aside all perceived obstacles, problems, or doubts, in order to give you freedom to imagine an ideal. It doesn't negate any difficult experience or circumstance, but it constructively shifts the focus of your attention and energy. You ask yourself, "If I could design any outcome here, if I could create any way out of this situation, what would that be?" This lens prioritizes *possibilities* over perceived *limits*. Then, once you have created the picture of the ideal, you can work backward to make it happen, applying an analytical or problem-solving lens as may be needed. (See **Creating the Reality You Want** on page 39.)

- **Opportunity lens.** With this lens, you ask yourself, "How can I find an opportunity in whatever situation I face?" For example, suppose the person next to you got promoted but you didn't, even though you felt you should have been. Most people would feel or say, "I can't believe that happened. That's not fair." Someone with an opportunity lens would have a very different perspective and instead ask, "How can I make sure that I get the *next* promotion?"

Impeding lenses:

- **"Problems to fix" or "what's wrong" lens.** With this lens, someone is always looking for something to go wrong; they are always wondering what *can* go wrong here, what *will* go wrong here? They focus on competitors and on the bad news. They never focus on opportunities in the same way. They can be successful, but not as successful as they could be given that they are prone to miss out on opportunities that this lens inhibits them from seeing.
- **Victim lens.** "It doesn't matter anyway." "I can't make a difference." "Bad things always happen to me." The picture is not accurate, but this person's belief is so strong that they make it a self-fulfilling prophecy. The energy to stop using this lens takes a lot more energy than staying within it.
- **Distrust/"It's not safe" lens.** A person with this lens operates from a default position that the world around them is inherently dangerous. They try to stay as safe as possible by initially viewing everyone and everything as a possible threat until proven otherwise. (See more on trust and distrust in Chapter 6).
- **Binary/"black or white" lens.** With this lens, a person tends to view situations as "either/or." There's no gray area, there's no middle ground. It's A or B, this or that. Black or white, one or two. No matter what arises for the individual in life or work, their lens reduces the nuances and myriad possibilities of reality into two simplistic (and often "opposing") buckets. (See more on engaging with multiple perspectives in Chapter 8.)

Each of these lenses has its own set of underlying beliefs and assumptions. Again, it's not that the core beliefs, or the perceptual lenses, are objectively right or wrong. In reality, sometimes they are accurate in a given situation, and inaccurate in another. But the bigger point is that you see what your lens shows you.

If you habitually default to the same lens all of the time, in every situation, then you are not perceiving the actual circumstances and environment around you. You are seeing only what your lens shows you. You are making assumptions instead of gleaning useful data that would more constructively guide your choices and actions.

You can't be human and be without any lenses, but you can be aware of your lens, as well as be intentional about choosing an appropriate lens for any given situation. There is a place for a competitive lens and a collaborative lens, for a problems lens and an opportunity lens, and so on. What does not serve us is to blindly and automatically apply one lens across the board no matter what is actually happening.

Your Perceptional Lenses Are Not *You*

Lenses begin to form when you are very young, and then strengthen and solidify over time. Every person's perceptual lenses have been shaped by many different influences in their life, both past and present. Some of the many influences include:

- Individual life experiences, especially early childhood
- Family history, norms, and expectations
- Ethnic or regional cultural norms and legacies
- Socioeconomic, religious, legal, and other institutional influences
- Exposure to media

The impacts of perceptual lenses play out in real life, often with huge consequences. That's why I am so passionate about making you pay attention to your perceptual lenses. They *often* fail to serve you. They can limit your performance, your potential, and your well-being. And not just you: they also fail to serve those around you, including the people at work who look to you for leadership and the people at home who care about you.

Please understand that the failing of your perceptual lens is not a failing of *you*. Your perceptual lenses are not who you are. They are just lenses that can come on and off. Like glasses, you can change them. You *need* to change them. And you will do that organically as you develop your mental fitness. Your reactiveness and feeling triggered will lesson and that will allow the real you to come forward.

Your capacity to be aware of the failures of your default perceptual lens—and to be able to change that lens—is the key to your personal and professional transformation in your performance at work, interpersonal relationships, and life. Mental fitness is all about increasing this capacity through intentional choices and application of skills. In developing mental fitness, you are going to learn how to access and understand your current (invisible to you) perceptual lenses, and you're going to learn how to change your perceptual lenses for the better.

Impeding beliefs lead to disempowered catabolic (negative) mood states. Helpful beliefs lead to empowered anabolic (positive) ones. As with all the muscles, we'll be diving into this much more deeply later. For now, just understand this mental fitness muscle involves *consciously choosing helpful beliefs versus impeding beliefs*.

CREATING THE REALITY YOU WANT: A STORY

Let's take a deeper dive on the **create possibility** lens. When you put on this lens you are designing the life you want. You look ahead and ask yourself, "What would be ideal?" Then, you work backward from there by asking, "What do I need to do to get where I want to be from where I am now?" I used this lens and process to transform myself and career from commodities trader to executive coach. Let me tell you how it came about.

One Friday after a day of trading I was riding home on the train. It was a beautiful day—one of the first nice days of summer in Chicago, but I was feeling a little depressed. I thought, What is wrong with me? I have a beautiful house. I have a good job. There was nothing outwardly wrong. But I was feeling melancholy. And I couldn't put my finger on why. I thought,

I know what I'll do. I'll get up really early tomorrow and head over to the coffee shop. I'll sit there, journal, and figure this out.

The next morning, staring at my nice, fresh clean pad of paper, I asked myself, "What's going on with me? What's not working in my life?"

The first thing I wrote down was how I hated having to get up with a 4:30 alarm every morning. "Damn, that sucks," I reflected. "I don't want to do that anymore. And you know what? I don't want to work five days a week, either. Four days a week—wouldn't that be nice?"

As soon as I wrote those things, I crumpled the paper and started to toss it. This is stupid. *Of course* you have to wake up to an alarm. *Of course* you're going to have to work five days a week. But as I was throwing my paper away, I heard a different voice within me saying, "No. The list is right. Keep going. Keep writing."

Some 232 items later—that's no exaggeration, I had written down everything big and small that annoyed me about my job and my life—well, now I felt even more depressed than I had before! But I directed myself to pay attention to all that I'd written. Clearly, there was something going on that needed to be addressed.

Next, I took a week off—it was a staycation—and I dealt with all the stuff on the list that I didn't like *and* that was within my control. These were things that had been annoying me for ages but that I hadn't done anything about. It ranged from cleaning out my bedroom closet and reorganizing my filing system to getting new heels for my favorite pair of shoes to scheduling a mammogram.

With those accomplished, I realized that a glaring number of items that remained on the list were work-related items. There were about thirty issues, such as, I don't like current company culture, and, I don't like that I can't control the number of meetings that I have to attend. As I looked over these final items, I realized there was no way most of these things could change unless I had my own company.

And, boom!

Suddenly I thought, Okay, if I *did* have a company, what would it be?

This process of trying to create the reality I wanted led me to conclude that for me to live the life I want, I needed to own my own company. My very next thought was: THIS IS CRAZY! I have no idea what kind of company to start! I just lost *all* my money in my last entrepreneurial venture! (My failed trading company.) Fortunately, as I started to feel despair, I had the self-awareness and presence of mind to look at the problem through a new lens—the create possibility lens. When I did that, I immediately felt different. In that moment, I was able to shift into ideation with excitement and passion.

I started to play with the idea. Okay, but *what if* I could create a new company? What would that company be? What would that look like? What would that feel like? What would I do? Right then and there I began a self-guided discovery process to discern what would be the greatest use of my talents. Then, I added another layer: how could I use my aptitude to provide the greatest value and service to others? Again, I honestly had no idea of the answer to any of the questions I was asking myself.

This self-directed exploratory process from "not knowing" to "knowing" took three years. Whenever I got discouraged, I adopted the create possibility lens and found myself continuing on with excitement and tenacity.

And, that's how it happened, my transition to executive coaching and the birth of Jody Michael Associates, my executive coaching company. That's what it looks like when you design your life. That's what it can look like when you tenaciously apply this particular lens.

This lens can work for you too, as it has for countless of my clients who have honed and tenaciously used this lens to create new future trajectories.

MUSCLE 3: SELF-ASSESS

This muscle is the skill of accurately self-assessing your internal state. What is your internal state? It's the running commentary in your head—your thoughts. It's also the moods and the emotions you feel and the physical sensations that you have, like a knot in your stomach. Self-assessing your internal state means that at any given moment you can observe yourself and articulate what you find.

Let's say that you are in a really bad mood. Well, that's vague. With mental fitness, you can say, for example, that you are experiencing a combination of disappointment, anger and anxiety, and a pounding headache. You can further identify the voice of your inner critic screaming: "You really screwed this one up big-time! See, you really *are* a fraud!"

If doing this kind of assessment seems like a lot to ask, don't worry: We have tools, processes, and technology to help. And the reward is very much worth the effort.

MUSCLE 4: HOLD MULTIPLE PERSPECTIVES

This skill is the ability to see multiple, disparate perspectives and viewpoints, and it shows up in different ways. One way is to understand and consider perspectives that are not in alignment with yours. If you've ever had a conversation about politics around the Thanksgiving table with your family, you know exactly what I am talking about. Typically, if you're like most people, you're focused on proving that your position is the *right* one. On the other hand, mental fitness allows you to hold multiple perspectives—appreciating and allowing for differences in opinions—so you leave the table without needing to establish who is right or wrong.

Another way of holding multiple, disparate perspectives is within yourself. With mental fitness, we replace either/or thinking with both/and. We acknowledge that two seemingly contradictory things can both be true at the same time. For example, we could be disappointed that our bid on a much-desired house was not accepted, *and* relieved because it would have been a somewhat risky financial stretch. We could be angry to learn that a loved one drove under the influence of alcohol, *and* also grateful that this time he arrived home safely and harmed no one.

We move beyond the simplicity of right/wrong, black/white, and either/or. We develop the skill of suspending judgment and embracing the complexity of gray and the potential of the yet-to-be-known.

MUSCLE 5: CALM YOUR PHYSIOLOGY

We typically underestimate the immense power we have over our physical state when we are distressed or upset in some way and to alter it in general. The fact is we can influence our own nervous systems. On the one hand, unhelpfully, we can easily intensify a catabolic state, such as "getting wound up." But helpfully, we can also calm ourselves, shifting from that catabolic to an anabolic state.

There are many techniques that are wildly effective—such as breathing exercises, biofeedback, and muscle relaxation—that you can use to quickly change your physical state when you are triggered or threatened. You'll be surprised at how quickly you can learn and apply them.

PERFORMANCE: ALL THE MUSCLES WORKING TOGETHER

Earlier, we used a sports analogy—making the pivotal free throw in a basketball game—to show how the result of training pays off in a moment of performance. It's the point at which all the developed muscles are working together in a systemic way so that you can achieve your objective.

In well-developed mental fitness, that moment of performance comes when you find yourself emotionally triggered. All five muscles work together seamlessly. In a very short span of time, you choose to own your distress; you calm your body; you self-assess your thoughts, moods, and physical sensations; you entertain and hold disparate perspectives; and finally, you let go of an impeding belief and instead choose a helpful one. Before we begin developing the five muscles in greater detail, we need to have a discussion about what can be getting in your way to creating mental fitness.

Key Points

- Mental fitness yields optimal performance. For you, **optimal performance means your mind is clear, sharp, and focused. You're using all of your brain for the issue at hand.**
- **Being mentally fit will not eliminate all the challenges in life.** Unfortunately, nothing can do that. But being mentally fit will allow you to deal with those challenges better, faster, and with less stress.
- **Mental fitness**, like physical fitness, **is measurable.**
- **Mental fitness is composed of five muscles.** Two choices—personal accountability and helpful versus impeding beliefs—and three skills—self-assessing your internal state, holding multiple perspectives, and moderating your physiology. You can flex each individually as well as holistically.

3

PINPOINTING THE PAIN

Q: Can you lead lightly if you are in pain?

A: No. If you're in pain, you're compromised physiologically and emotionally. You're suffering. So no, you really can't lead lightly if you are in pain.

However, pain is a fantastic catalyst because it is the spark that can get you to change. But you won't change unless you acknowledge the pain in the moment. So, it turns out that pain is a great thing because it gives you the signal that it is time to practice going against your normal way of doing things, the way that is causing you problems. This is the moment where you have an opportunity to start to shape your brain to respond differently, to refocus your perceptual lenses to see differently.

Eliminating the pain will make it possible to lead lightly. Otherwise, you are living in a state of stress, being overwhelmed and frustrated.

Mental fitness has multiple benefits. It will eliminate many of the roadblocks you are putting—perhaps unconsciously—in front of yourself. It will allow you to function at a higher level than you are now, and it will make you a better leader. But perhaps its biggest advantage is simply this: it will move you from pain to performance.

We will talk about pain here. And in the next chapter we can then talk about how you can create performance. But we need to address where you are first: *Are you in pain?*

I'm not talking about your aching muscles from yesterday's CrossFit workout. I'm talking about *you*, your mental state. *How are you, really?* And while we're at it, what about your direct reports and peers? Are they in pain? Is your organization in pain?

You're not alone if you hate these questions. They're uncomfortable to think about. We've all been taught that in the workplace, pain is taboo. I see that when I go into corporations and talk to executives about pain. At best, I will get a cautious acknowledgement of its existence, but if that happens— and again, it's rare—it's usually in a private "offline" conversation. Mostly I see (and face) intense resistance and a physiological response to the discussion. I can't read their minds, but I can read their body language. They do not want to talk about it.

Pain is a taboo subject among executives and organizations. Rarely do workplace discussions about emotions or moods take place. This is true despite the fact that emotions and moods profoundly impact individual and team performance as well as organizational culture.

But here's the thing: In all my years of executive coaching, I have yet to meet a person in corporate America today who does *not* have recurring complaints about something in their day-to-day work experience. Perhaps they have a difficult colleague. Or can't get stakeholders on board. Their workload is unfair and no one recognizes their efforts. Their boss makes lousy decisions. On it goes. Oh, there is plenty to complain about.

Take a moment to realize that whenever you complain, *that's an example of pain.* Maybe you don't call it that. In the corporate setting, we have more acceptable words. We say it's *stress.* Or *irritation, frustration, worry.*

How odd that executives easily talk about a business's "pain points," but as soon as I mention *people* being in pain, it's like the hot potato no one wants to touch. To many, personal pain implies weakness.

If people are forced to confront personal pain in the organization—because of an employee "issue," for example—they punt it as soon as possible to HR (who really don't want it, either). In my many years of working with executives at all levels and across all industries I have found one thing to be consistently true: people are in a lot of pain. Some know it but try to mask it. Many others don't even know they are in pain—and will deny it when asked because it may not register. For people who keep themselves going all the time—Type As—it's like pain is the water they are swimming in; they don't recognize it for what it is because it's the only way they have ever known.

Even worse, pain multiplies upon itself. People in pain unknowingly create additional pain for those around them, and for their organizations. Here's a typical example. Usually, the person in pain is a driver. They're constantly focused on *doing* (executing), on doing *more*, relentlessly without taking a breath—taxing their physiology limits and keeping their lens focused primarily on the tactical. All the while, they are missing the importance of reading the individual or the room, developing strategy, prioritizing, creating followership, or navigating with nuanced situational leadership.

That can cause three specific problems. The first is communication. Concerned that explaining things in detail will slow down getting the work done, they probably are not going to give adequate context for what they want done, which is frustrating for the people who work for them because there are going to be a lot of do-overs. These direct reports won't always do the right thing, because they can't discern what the right thing is. Second, these drivers are going to err toward being directive rather than inspiring, because they're focused solely on results. And finally, they are not going to be nurturing or empathetic, because they don't feel there is any time for that either. As a result, the people working for them are not going to feel appreciated or heard, nor are they being set up for success.

Whether you're aware of your pain or not, that pain compromises your energy, limits what's possible for you, and—last but not least—heavily damages your performance and potentially others' performance as well.

As I've said, my firsthand experience with leaders teaches me that they are in a lot of pain, both recognized and unrecognized. Different kinds of pain, yes; but pain nonetheless. Think about it. How many people do you know—coworkers, friends, family, neighbors—who actually love their job? Who feel blessed to be doing what they do every day? The graphic here, from a survey done by Gallup, shows the number is remarkably small. Only 31 percent of employees are actively engaged.

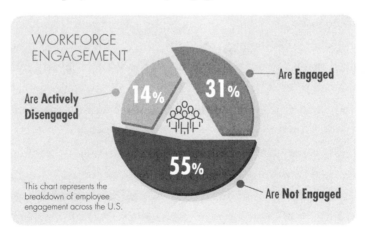

WORKFORCE ENGAGEMENT

Are **Actively Disengaged**

14%

31%

Are **Engaged**

55%

Are **Not Engaged**

This chart represents the breakdown of employee engagement across the U.S.

And while that 14 percent actively disengaged figure doesn't look so bad, as Gallup was quick to point out, that means the remaining 55 percent are not engaged; they are psychologically unattached to their work and company. These employees put time, but not energy or passion, into their work.[1]

---

1 Source: Jim Harter, "Historic Drop in Employee Engagement Follows Record Rise," Gallup Workplace, July 2, 2020, https://www.gallup.com/workplace/313313/historic-drop-employee-engage-ment-follows-record-rise.aspx

Why am I pushing so hard on this point? Because I get hired to transform leaders and help them achieve dramatically higher levels of performance *no matter* how stressful or difficult their personal or professional circumstances. And what I know is that **pain hinders performance.** So, if you want to play at the top of your game, if you want to be an outstanding leader, if you want to create even higher levels of success in your organization, then you have to do two things: One, stop the cycle of pain. Two, shift into a cycle of performance.

Making that shift is a fundamental, essential skill. I am going to show you how to practice it.

THREAT AND EMOTION

Some years ago, I put myself in a total and complete state of panic. My mind was racing wildly. My palms were sweaty. Even worse, I could barely catch my breath. The world was rapidly collapsing in on me and my mind and **body screamed** in unison: "Danger! Danger!! *Danger!!!*"

I was not being robbed at gunpoint. I was not trapped in a burning building. What was my big problem? I was about four hours away from going up onstage to participate in a panel discussion. And I was absolutely terrified. This made no sense. I *loved* speaking before executive groups and had been doing so for two decades. And yet, I was in a full-fledged state of fight or flight.

The panel topic was negotiation. The audience would include reporters from a variety of industries and media. I did not consider myself to be even remotely an expert on this topic. I didn't belong there. The reporters would see that—reporters ask tough questions! My panic ensued. Why had I accepted this offer? What had I been thinking?

Well, I will tell you exactly what. A cherished former client had offered me the opportunity. At the time, I was grateful to be asked but had politely declined, saying that I lacked the expertise. But my client had pushed back, flattering me in the process. She said my coaching had made her a more powerful negotiator, which helped her land a six-figure book deal.

She continued, "And, how about my friend, too? Your salary negotiation coaching helped her double her salary during the interview process.

Obviously, you are qualified and will be just great." My ego took the bait! I felt good about the whole thing, put in on my calendar, and didn't give it another thought.

It wasn't until the day of the event, after I finished with my last client, that I realized what a horrible mistake I had made. I was going to be on stage in just four hours.

As panic took hold, it was clear what I had to do: I had to learn *every-thing* that was *ever* written about negotiation. *Now!* In the precious few hours before start time, I could become an expert on the topic. I went into a frenzy of activity. I thought to myself:

> OK, I got this. I'm smart, I'll figure this out. I'm sure there's a frame-work for negotiation. I'll just go on Wikipedia, find the framework, learn it, memorize it. No problem. OK, here's Wikipedia . . . here's the negotiation page . . . wait, what? There are how many negotiation frameworks? Four! No. Five? Ack! How am I supposed to know which one is the best? I can't tell! OK, I'll pick this one. It had better be this one!

If you had been a fly on the wall, you would have seen me intensely focused, concentrating, studying, memorizing. And I stayed like that for about forty-five minutes. But on the inside—the part you couldn't have seen—I was panic-stricken.

You know that feeling you get when you first know that you've gotten sick, and you can feel your whole body crashing? I suddenly felt that horrible feeling. With my body screaming at me, my thoughts went wild.

> Oh my god, I am getting sick! This is terrible! I can't believe it! Wait, no, it's not terrible. Oh, this is *great*. Yes! I'm sick, I can cancel! Oh thank god, it's legit! I don't have to go up there on that stage. *No, you idiot, you cannot cancel*, that would be terrible for your personal brand, your reputation. You can't bail on this. It's too important. What the hell are you thinking?

And in that moment—sick and exhausted—I stopped. I just stopped. I knew better. This was not me. I had just made myself sick. I took several deep breaths to clear my mind and took my thinking in a new direction: *What's the best thing I can do, right now, to be my best self on that stage?*

I realized that the very best thing to do was to sleep and restore myself. I lay down, set an alarm for ninety minutes, and was asleep within five.

When I awoke, I remembered my best self: I'm good on my feet. I am someone who consistently performs well under pressure whether on the trading floor or a stage. I had never experienced humiliation in a professional setting, why would that start now? Furthermore, I knew that if I didn't know an answer while up on stage, I could simply turn to another panelist and invite them to answer instead.

What was my mindset as I showed up for the discussion? "I am going to crush it."

You know the ending of the story, of course. The event turned out to be easy and pleasurable. It was all fine. *Of course.* I was relaxed and present throughout, and I received positive feedback for my contributions to a successful panel.

WHAT WAS MY PROBLEM?

What was this panic all about? I was deeply, emotionally *triggered.*

We all have places where we are emotionally vulnerable. My personal brand and reputation—and those of my company—have always been extremely important to me. In my mind, this panel event was presenting me to the public in a way that might have jeopardized something that I cared about so deeply. That is what created the emotional trigger for me. Physiologically, I slid into an intensely *catabolic* (destructive) state.

This was pain that *I created.* No external factor caused it. I did it completely on my own! In fact, this is what people do to themselves all day long: create their own pain. This is exactly what I want people—what I want *you*—to stop doing. I want you to stop creating these energy-draining moods. Stop being a victim. As for me, I managed to stop it when I realized that imagining the worst-case scenario was "creating" my anxiety. Once I knew that, I could then take the more helpful actions of renewing myself through sleep and focusing on my authentic self.

We're all going to have pain in life—me, you, everyone. And when that pain is real, you want to be able to manage that pain effectively. But you don't want to create pain unnecessarily, the way I did in worrying about being on the panel. There's a whole lot of pain in life being created unnecessarily by people who don't realize that they are creating it.

As human beings we all get triggered. It's normal. Whether the threat is real or self-inflicted (as it was in my case with the panel discussion) the underlying physiological response of the mind and body is always the same: fight, flight, or freeze.

And therein lies our opportunity to stop the cycle of pain, and shift instead to a new, powerful cycle of *performance*. I think you will agree that if I had stayed in that catabolic state, if I had gone up to the stage and sat terrified on the panel with my mind stuffed with panicked Wikipedia facts, I could not possibly have performed well.

Let's talk about why being on stage in a catabolic state would have been a disaster and how we can make the shift from pain to performance happen.

Amygdala and Prefrontal Cortex

When triggered, your brain's **amygdala** is activated. The amygdala is an older part of the brain. From an evolutionary standpoint, our long-ago ancestors stayed alive through the amygdala's hypervigilant sensitivity to threats in the environment.

Even today, an activated amygdala *immediately* shifts you into fight, flight, or freeze. You literally lose access to the rational processing power of your brain's **prefrontal cortex**.

The amygdala drives you to defend, react, protect, withdraw, or aggress towards the perceived threat. Unfortunately, your amygdala cannot distinguish between a hungry, angry grizzly bear and a self-induced fear of your CEO's probing questions about your project metrics.

MindMastery retrains your brain's habits. You learn to *override* the amygdala, and re-engage and strengthen your rational, prefrontal cortex. To create performance instead of pain!

CATABOLISM AND ANABOLISM

Let's begin with a couple of quick definitions that build on what we introduced in the last chapter. Your body has two main physiological states: catabolic and anabolic. Bruce D. Schneider, in his book *Energy Leadership*, was the first to apply these terms to energetic states. Catabolic is painful and destructive energy. Anabolic is the good stuff; it's energy that is healing and restorative. Schneider's theory of seven levels of energy has influenced me greatly, and I'd highly recommend reading his book to learn more.

The more you learn about these states, the more you may become aware that much of the time you are suffering on your automatic pilot. A catabolic state is probably your default. Your awareness of your catabolic state is the first step in making the crucial shift to consistently better performance regardless of what the day may throw at you.

But first, let's talk about catabolic energy itself. This is your body's way of responding to a survival threat, i.e., you need to get out of this burning building *now!* Catabolic energy gives you a short burst of very intense, very powerful physical energy. Not that caffeine jolt from the Red Bull that you chug at 11:00 PM as you agonize over the details of tomorrow's presentation to your board of directors. I'm talking about the extreme energy your body needs when a very large hungry predator is hell-bent on devouring your flesh. That's when you need to flee as fast as you can, or attack with unerring accuracy. If you fail at either, it's truly game over.

Granted, there are no ravenous lions, tigers, or bears at work. However, your body will respond to *any* stressor—minor or major, real or imagined—with that kind of catabolic energy. When I was panicking about my panel discussion, of course there was no predator, no *actual* threat to my physical safety. I was safe in my office. But it didn't matter, because my mind perceived the situation as severely threatening. Not the destruction of my physical body, but of my professional reputation. That's how catabolic energy works. When the mind perceives *any* type of threat—actual or perceived—your body will respond in the only way it knows: by producing catabolic energy. I can't emphasize this enough.

The body does not distinguish between a real threat and an imagined one. It responds the same no matter what.

The problem is, while catabolic energy has an important (and primal) survival purpose, ultimately it hurts you when it is ongoing, day after day, week after week, month after month. It negatively impacts your body and your mental state. It is draining and depleting. In this condition, how can you consistently perform at your best? You can't.

Here's a simple analogy. Catabolic energy is like a blender at high speed. For the short term, it's great. Your blender does what it is supposed to do—quickly. But keeping the blender on high, long term, uses up a tremendous amount of energy. Eventually the blender (and your body) wears down.

What You Need to Know About: Catabolic Energy

Catabolic energy releases massive amounts of chemicals and hormones to help you overcome a short-term immediate threat, but when they are constant—instead of short lived—you damage your immune system. In this book, and in JMA's coaching, we use this same idea to also describe a person's mood state and energy presentation: catabolic energy means the individual is in a state of stress or pain.

In everyday language, what we call *stress* is a catabolic state. Stress is a factor in five out of the six leading causes of death—heart disease, cancer, stroke, respiratory disease, and accidents—according to the University of

California Medical School's Dr. Peter Schnall, an expert on the role occupational stress plays in our lives.

Very simply, catabolic energy is pain and suffering. Most people are in the throes of catabolic energy. I don't mean once in a while—like my temporary terror prior to my speaking event. I mean *in the majority of their waking hours.* They're not even aware of it! Why? Because it's their norm. It is what they've been feeling for months—or even years. That's why I say it is their default operating state. Of course, people experience different levels of pain, but regardless of the intensity, the underlying mood state is still catabolic. Annoyed or enraged, concerned or scared, mildly embarrassed or humiliated—it is all catabolic.

If you rarely experience dramatic negative moods, you might conclude that none of this applies to you. I completely disagree. For one thing, it is very common for many people to feel nothing (neither bad nor good) because they are in a catabolic state of being numb or "checked out." I'm talking about avoiding. Not dealing. Dissociating. You shove down everything that is bothering you, but it doesn't go away. You just move it to the subconscious and unconscious. You do that often enough, and sooner or later you may experience a panic attack. And even when catabolic energy is at lower intensity levels, if it remains chronic over time, it still causes serious and lasting damage to the body.

CATABOLIC LEADERS IN THE WORKPLACE

Organizations are filled with people in pervasive catabolic energy states. Their daily performance is suboptimal and negatively affects others. The higher the leadership level, the worse the impact. As we saw earlier in the chapter, a catabolic executive unknowingly creates unintended consequences that ripple out throughout the entire business.

What does a catabolic leader look like? In a moment, I'll invite you to examine some composite senior executive profiles based on my coaching career. Taken together, these profiles represent a large number of leaders I have worked with or encountered.

But first, a caution. I'm not prone to labeling people or putting them into neat little diagnostic boxes. I prefer not to use assessments that tell you who you are, such as "You are an ENTJ," as the Myers-Briggs assessment might say. I believe it is disempowering to tell someone "you are *this*" or "you are *that*." Labels imply people cannot change. That is completely contrary to my experience. People *can* change. People *do* change. I've seen it again and again.

When I make an observation such as "Your energy is catabolic right now," or "You are displaying unproductive catabolic behavior," it is not who you *are*. Understand that your catabolic energy is simply your temporary *state* at that moment. This can be really hard to understand at first, since you probably know your catabolic state so well that you will likely think it is you. But that's just because it is so familiar. But it's still not *you*.

So, with all that said: The following profiles of catabolic leaders are meant to describe *tendencies only*; behaviors and results that are often seen together. As you read them, notice what pain is being created. How is the executive suffering? How are their peers and direct reports suffering? How is the organization as a whole suffering?

In fact, I'd like you to read each profile two times:

1. On the first read, what do you recognize from your own company or past workplaces? The profiles may not be an exact match, but note what is familiar to you.
2. The second read is going to be more challenging. Read each profile as if someone has written it about *you*. Which aspects of these profiles might we see in you sometimes? *No judgment.* We're just building awareness.

Driving Dave

"Driving Dave" is the most common profile of the high-level executives whom I coach. Driving Dave is a superstar. When it comes to driving results for the company, he is the best performer around—a ten out of ten! He prides himself on his capacity to work harder than anyone. Call him a workaholic, and he'll proudly agree. He gets a great rush from moving fast, delivering fast. It's almost an adrenaline addiction and he's always going for that fix.

It's all great except for one important thing: while he's a ten at driving results, he's often only a five with people. Whenever there is a problem, he quickly looks to find fault with others. No one is quick enough, smart enough, or performs well enough. He's surrounded by people who are not as fast or effective, and they create obstacles to rapid progress. He's impatient with them and often irritable.

Rarely does Driving Dave take the time to coach or develop his direct reports. Often he thinks, "It's easier and faster to just do it myself," and so he does. As a result, he gets in the way of developing his people and leveraging his team. At the extreme, he can be unreasonable in his expectations. His leadership communication style is directive; he primarily gives orders.

To summarize: Driving Dave's overarching lens is "profits over people." He displays little to no empathy; he thinks of his people as "resources" and has no understanding of them as individuals. His focus is always on immediate performance: Check things off the list. Move things forward at lightning speed. Apply pressure when and where necessary. Never let up on the gas. As a result, Dave is often unable to build or create sustained followership. People leave, fantasize about leaving, or are actively pursuing a new job.

Do you recognize elements of Driving Dave? Take a moment to consider the following questions and jot down some thoughts.

1. What is Driving Dave's impact on the people who work for him? What do they feel? What pain do they have?

2. What is Driving Dave's impact on the overall organization? What organizational pain does his behavior create?

3. Perhaps most important, what might be Driving Dave's own pain?

Here's what I see when I see Driving Dave.

Driving Dave's Impact on Others

Among the people who work for him, Driving Dave elicits widespread feelings of inadequacy and "it's never good enough." His people are constantly worked to exhaustion. He damages the company's brand on social media when word spreads, and good people don't want to join his organization, fearing he is representative of all the managers there.

To be clear, Dave is *not* the supportive type of leader who sets high standards and then intentionally pushes his people to develop in a way that feels good and right. Rather, his people become a tribe of the overwhelmed, seeking comfort from each other. They bond in the same way that siblings in dysfunctional families often do: they manage their pain by supporting each other. Plus, they stay in their job longer than they should because they are physically and emotionally depleted; they don't have the energy or time to embark upon a job hunt.

But there are a couple of Dave's direct reports who experience him differently. You see, Dave picks favorites; high performers with strong intrinsic motivation not to disappoint anyone (especially their leader). While these favorites may be tired and overworked, they don't have the same feelings of never-good-enough. They feel appreciated.

Driving Dave's Impact on the Organization's Pain Points

Although Driving Dave hits his numbers, there is way too much collateral damage. His leadership is unbalanced; it's too heavily skewed on driving results without building followership. His people are neither aligned, inspired, nor loyal. Cross-functional peers find it painful to work with him because Dave has a single-minded focus on his own agenda. As a result, there is much less collaboration to achieve shared goals than there could be. Rather, there is distrust as colleagues find countless ways to avoid having to work with Dave.

Driving Dave's Own Pain Point

In the early and middle part of his career, Driving Dave is aggressively promoted. Fast-moving, highly competitive industries like finance and technology will tolerate a leader like Dave, and at times he does make it to the top there, but typically he hits a hard stop because of all the leadership gaps we've mentioned. When that happens, over and over, his best people leave. And, if they don't leave, quite frankly, they should! Dave wreaks havoc on their health and quality of life.

Driving Dave is just one example of a catabolic executive. Here are some brief descriptions of others.

Overwhelmed Olivia

Overwhelmed Olivia is a high performer who is absolutely exhausted and running on empty. Although extremely capable, she feels like she is drinking from a fire hose, barely keeping up. She repeatedly misses precious family time in order to catch up on work. In fact, she often says, "If I just go in on Saturday I can catch up, and then I'll be fine going forward." She begins the week feeling excited and optimistic because she is all caught up, but by the end of the week she's in exactly the same place again.

Blaming Brad

Poor Brad! Through no fault of his own, he will tell you: He was passed over for promotion, his boss doesn't appreciate him, and his direct reports fail him more often than he'd like. That plum initiative he wanted to head up? It goes to someone else, every time.

Brad has myriad explanations about why nothing ever works out, everything from "he never had a mentor" to "no one knows" how hard he works.

But he never asks himself what he might be doing that is ineffective. He's not introspective. In fact, it's likely he's so defensive and guarded, he won't even admit to himself there are opportunities for his development. His team is certainly not going to be inspired because his primary lens is "Woe is me" or "woe is us."

Things are hard for Brad. And they stay hard because he doesn't know how to change. He doesn't even realize that he needs to change to achieve what he wants—he's just waiting on everyone else to change around him.

Rigid Roger

Rigid Roger absolutely knows he's right. He has developed subject matter expertise, deeply trusting only his own view because he has honed it and honed it over the years. His thinking is rigidly black-and-white and he avoids anything gray (it feels out of control to him).

While Roger has previously enjoyed success as an individual contributor, now he is a leader and has a real problem. He is forced to rely on other people to get things done, but he doesn't easily trust. He is not effective at delegating and generally holds on to too much himself. When he does delegate, he often pokes, prods, and bullies others to try to get them to deliver better and faster than his superiors expect, so that he can continue to be seen as performing well.

Fearful Frank

Fearful Frank suffers from analysis paralysis. He won't make a decision unless he has 100 percent of the data. He doesn't want to be wrong. He doesn't want to make a mistake. He's a trend follower and a safety seeker; as a leader he stays behind the scenes when he should be out in front.

Frank is driven by his internal fears but he doesn't want anyone to know. He is tight, guarded, and reticent, but he is adept at posturing. To avoid putting skin in the game, he adopts a style of openly questioning everything ("Do you think that is the right choice?") without ever taking an actual stance. He tries to get others to make—or at least share ownership of—the decision. His behavior creates contradictions in the room, leaving people confused and the process bottlenecked.

That last point is important. Obviously, there is a huge cost to Frank's inaction. In the hypercompetitive world we all operate in, he is a drag on the organization's ability to make a decision. He is not a nimble speedboat. Getting him to move is like trying to change the direction of an ocean liner. He will change, but his changing of direction will be laborious and slow compared to people around him.

Checked-Out Cherie

Checked-out Cherie has given up. She's keeping the seat warm at work, but that's about it. She has low energy; she's not engaged with any level of enthusiasm or creativity. Why bother, she asks. Work is always the same old, same old.

On her best days Cherie just feels resigned. On her worst, she feels despair and hopelessness. Her leader is frustrated with her lack of engagement, and her peers find it easier to work around her than with her. It's not uncommon for Cherie to show up as emotionally flat, or for her to embody a negative or complaining demeanor.

In these profiles, what do you recognize from your own company or past workplaces? Which aspects of these profiles might someone see in you sometimes? How would you answer the questions in the box on page 57 for those that ring the most familiar?

THE COSTS OF CATABOLIC ENERGY

For an organization, the executive pain in all the leaders we just talked about is the most expensive pain of all. Each leader's every behavior or action (or lack thereof) ripples up, down, and across the org chart. Most people can sense this, and it shows up tangibly in the comments in 360 feedback, negative social media (Glassdoor, Blind) comments, high employee attrition, low engagement, and an absence of nominations and wins in "Best Places to Work" roundups.

Executive communication, mood, and behavior set the tone and form the basis of the organization's culture.

To some degree these negative, costly impacts are no secret to organizations. That's why "employee engagement" is such a buzzword today. It's why companies spend billions to survey their employees, tweak their incentive frameworks, implement new training programs, and roll out ambitious new "culture" initiatives. But consultative, organizational design and human resource approaches often miss the point.

True, their solutions usually represent the best practices that should be effective. And actually, these solutions *would* be effective, if they were applied to organizations filled with mentally fit employees and leaders. But mostly, that's not what we have. Our organizations are filled with stressed, overwhelmed, anxious, exhausted people. That includes the very same HR leaders and other professionals who are trying to address the systemic problems of disengagement and underperformance!

CHECKING THE BOXES IS NOT ALWAYS THE WAY TO GO

Last year I had the fascinating—yet jarring—experience of being evaluated by two different physicians. I wasn't having any dramatic physical symptoms, but I had not been feeling at my best for some time. Something felt "off," so I wanted to check my overall physical health and identify and address any problems head on.

So I went to see my regular doctor, a smart, Harvard-trained individual with a great bedside manner. He had impeccable credentials and reputation, and he had been my physician for years. He ran all the usual tests and said, "Jody, everything checked out fine. You're in good shape. Your metabolic panel, vitamins, and minerals are in the normal range. Your cholesterol is a tad high, but nothing worrisome. I wouldn't put you on a statin for it. Overall, there's nothing broken here. Good job." I left feeling pretty good, like I had just gotten an A-minus report card on my health.

But about a week later, I read a book on functional medicine that shook me to my core. Functional medicine overlaps with traditional medicine in many ways, but it takes a systemic approach to identifying and treating the root causes of illnesses and disease. I saw that I had been using a very limited scorecard for my health, where "fine" meant no diseases were found and nothing was "broken." But this book showed me that I was not managing my health from a *systemic perspective*. I began to completely re-evaluate my approach to my health.

I went to see a functional medicine physician, telling him, "Give me every test you think is important so that I can maximize my current and future health." He did the same standard tests as my regular physician, plus a lot more that would indicate how well my biological system was functioning right down to the mitochondria (cellular) level.

What he found wasn't good. My mercury levels were four times higher than normal. My arsenic levels were twice as high as they should be. A whole host of other toxic metals, such as lead and cadmium, were also at alarmingly high levels. If left untreated, these levels of toxicity can lead to neurological breakdowns and disease. Nutritionally, the news was no better. Even though I was dutifully eating a healthy, organic diet, my body was not absorbing enough of the vitamins and minerals from these foods due to the elevated toxins.

After going over the test results, this physician told me, "Jody, it doesn't look so good. There are issues here that have been in the making for a long time. You will need to take immediate steps and also make longer-term proactive changes if you want to be at your healthiest in the coming years." Essentially, his grade of my health was a D, at best!

Wait, *what*?

How could I get such vastly different results from two highly qualified experts who were equal in their credentials, pedigrees, and reputations? The core difference was in their *perspectives*. It was a perfect illustration of what I call "checking the boxes"—a counterproductive approach that I see in organizations all the time.

My original physician had based his assessment on data from the standard panel of tests. He had checked all the boxes: Blood labs, check. Vitals, check. Reflexes, check. Weight, could be better, check. No symptoms, check. No problems, check.

He found nothing out of the ordinary in the areas in which he looked, and therefore said I was fine. Although standard, this is a superficial measure of health that will only identify problems that have already strongly manifested in the body. This physician did nothing wrong, but what he did wasn't enough. He wasn't focused on achieving my optimal health or preventing illnesses and diseases in my future.

The second physician, who said my health needed immediate attention, based his assessment on a much broader and more detailed set of tests. It was a completely different process designed to answer questions such as: "Is Jody performing at her best? Is there any unseen damage occurring to her system? Is there any suboptimal functioning in one part of her physiological system that is negatively impacting other parts? If she changes nothing today, what is her health prognosis ten years ahead?" He took a systemic approach and his treatment plan was detailed and comprehensive.

NEEDED: A SYSTEMATIC APPROACH

In my work as an executive coach, I take a systemic perspective of both individuals and organizations. When companies approach me to work with their leadership, I seek to understand and address the organization's *systemic* problems—the root causes—to create real and sustained change. That means dealing with the underlying and often unseen executive pain and transforming persistent catabolic (negative) energy that hurts the individual leader and the company.

But unfortunately, most companies typically want coaching that's easy, fast, and painless for all involved. From my perspective, they are just checking the boxes. Find an executive coach! (Check.) Get that coach on board! (Check.) Executive gets coached! (Check.) Okay, coaching's done! (Nope.) With some tactical coaching, the executive's behavior might improve to a degree, but it most likely won't be sustainable. If new challenges arise, or the current challenges intensify, those superficial improvements often do not hold. That's why we need to take a systemic approach.

But frankly, this systemic lens can be a tough sell. Excavating and doing the deep work, while the return on investment might be great, just isn't as sexy or expedient. Think about all the podcasts and blogs out there that promise a quick fix (with a minimal amount of effort) to change your life, leadership, productivity, etc. They abound.

But even though a superficial approach may be an easier pill to swallow, or bring apparent quick results, that does not make them an effective or sustainable solution. Superficial fixes are simply not my way or my organization's way to transform leaders; they never have been. And in my opinion, they shouldn't be *your* way! Not if you want to make truly profound change in your life, your work, or your organization.

WHAT PERFORMANCE LOOKS LIKE

Despite the prevalence of catabolic energy in the workplace, you have the capacity to actively manage yourself in a way that creates, and maintains, anabolic energy. When you learn to do that for the majority of your waking hours, the result is consistent *performance*. You can completely transform yourself through mental fitness.

As you recall, anabolic energy is the "good stuff" where your body is in a mode of repairing and restoring, building itself back up. There is no constant cascade of stress hormones and no energy depletion, because there will be fewer perceived threats or danger.

What will life and work be like when you are mentally fit? It is not an exaggeration to say: **EVERYTHING WILL BE DIFFERENT**.

Yes, *everything*. I know that's a bold statement. You probably cannot imagine what "different" looks like when every day feels like the same crappy thing over and over. Change can seem abstract, and maybe even unattainable. Given that good role models are difficult to find, I'm going to paint a picture for you. It's going to be a picture of *you*, once you have developed greater mental fitness.

Ask the skeptical part of you to step aside for just a little bit, and just read and think about the following passage without judgment.

> With mental fitness, you're Teflon. It doesn't matter what is being thrown at you, day after day; it doesn't stick to you.
> When you're Teflon, you're not reactive. You don't feel threatened. You don't feel triggered. Your body and mind do not constantly flip into

fight-or-flight mode. You see the drama outside of you, but it is like watching a play. You're watching attentively, but it's not punching you in the gut. You're able to have that centered space inside of you where the drama does not impact you.

When you are Teflon, so much more has become possible:

You Have Full Capacity of Your Brain

You're present in the moment. You can make solid decisions. Why? Because the executive functioning and decision-making region of your brain isn't compromised. You're not rigid in your thinking, and you are able to actively listen to different perspectives.

You're Not Wasting Valuable Energy in Distress

You are managing your energy well instead of feeling depleted and overwhelmed. As a result, you're able to maintain optimal performance.

You Are High Functioning in Your Interpersonal Communications and Relationships

Interpersonally, you "dance" well with others. You can avoid explosive land mines, because you come to everything with curiosity and a desire to understand instead of a need to defend, to be right, and to attack or defend yourself when provoked or challenged.

With mental fitness you are able to do all of this *consistently*—not just on your good days or once in a while when all the conditions are just right.

Perhaps most significant, you can do all of this when you are emotionally triggered. Yes, you absolutely will get triggered; you're human. But you'll get out of that triggered state in minutes, or maybe even seconds—not hours, not days, not weeks.

THE JOYS AND LIMITATIONS OF "JUST DO IT"

Sometimes when I talk about changing from pain to performance, people say, "I get it. I need to change. As the folks at Nike say, 'Just Do It.'" My response to that is yes, but with a caveat.

"Just do it" is a very powerful phrase. If you are going to have a mantra in life, it is one of the best, because it eliminates all the excuses. You feel tired and don't want to work out? Well, the response to that is "just do it; just work out anyway."

However, "just do it" is not very mindful. And it primarily has an external focus. If all you say is "just do it," you are not asking yourself reflective questions like "Why am I doing it?" "Do I understand the benefit of doing it?" "What could I be doing differently?" "What else could I be doing that is more effective and beneficial?"

Let me give you an example. I worked with a leader years ago, and he was like a commando when it comes to "just do it." This guy was the best at it. At the end of the week, he'd look back and evaluate, "How much did I get done? How fast did I get it done?"

In coaching, I had to say to him, "Listen, you're a partner in the firm. You've got to stop applying this lens and measuring your progress by how much you got accomplished. You're asking the wrong questions. You're asking entry-level questions."

We worked on asking better, more meaningful, strategic questions. He started to slow down and contemplate more. He built a long-term strategy that drove better near-term and long-term results. He prioritized, instead of merely knocking things off his teams' to-do list. He started to engage in more impactful conversations all across the company. Yes, he still has a "just do it" approach. But now he is doing things that really matter.

In essence, he slowed down to speed up. As a result, he became a more powerful leader with greater impact. He married "Just Do It" with complimentary strategy and thoughtfulness.

PAINTING A MORE DETAILED PORTRAIT

When you are mentally fit, you are not ruminating or stewing. You are not stuck dwelling on what's wrong or what could go wrong—thoughts that impede your performance. Instead, you're resilient. You don't take things personally. Whatever people may say to you slides right off of you.

On those rare occasions when you do find yourself triggered or threatened, it's just momentary. You quickly regain your emotional equilibrium. In fact, when things do go wrong—the first place you look is *you*. Not to others! You're not looking to blame. Instead, you're looking to understand, to solve, to resolve.

When you are mentally fit, your thoughts, moods, and behaviors are not obstacles in the way of your success. This alignment increases the very probability that you will, in fact, succeed!

When you're mentally fit, you are not stuck. You move forward. You're flexible. You listen, and you're open to new ideas that aren't your own. As a result, you and the stakeholders around you are more energized and engaged. Does all this sound too idyllic? Stop that thinking right now. There was a time in my life when I did not understand any of this either.

As a child, life was often hard and chaotic, and always unstable. Too frequently I knew poverty, even hunger, the brutality of repeated abuse, and the terrible heartache of watching my mother go in and out of institutions for years with intractable mental illness. I came out of all this as a young adult who was strong, ambitious, and visionary . . . but also emotionally reactive, quick to temper, and absolutely miserable inside. At the time, I managed my volatile moods by finding healthy emotional release—first as a competitive athlete in high school (basketball, volleyball, track, and tennis) and college (basketball, volleyball, softball), and then later as a trader on the floor of the Chicago Mercantile Exchange where aggressive behavior worked in my favor. Over time, I began to find professional success.

By all outward appearances, I had it all together. Inwardly, it was a different story. My emotional turmoil was intolerable. I had unhealthy levels of anxiety and dysfunctional relationships. Over and over, my behavior threatened to derail the hard-won success I was creating. Even though I was a natural leader, I was well on my way to becoming the type of catabolic leader that, years later, I would coach. Yes, I was *that* person.

However, I cared too much about my future to give up. I was driven by a growth mindset—the fundamental belief that I had the power and capability within me to change. I desperately wanted to be out of pain and to create a better life and a better me. So, I started to work on myself. Relentlessly. I found self-help books and workshops. Motivational speakers. Spiritual development groups. And I went through deep, intense psychoanalysis. I did all of this because I instinctively understood one fundamental thing about myself: my thoughts, moods, and behavior were driven by the deficits I had experienced in my childhood, but they had nothing to do with *who I actually was*. The core and essence of my being were none of these things.

I tell you all of this so that you understand when we talk about mental fitness, I am not teaching you a *theory*. I am coaching you to use what works in the real world, in your real environment, with whatever real background is part of your life to date. I know, intimately, what it's like to be doing the best you can, while at the same time unwittingly sabotaging yourself. It is because I have lived this path that I can break the taboo about executive pain and speak about its dire costs. Most important, I can say with full confidence that extraordinary change is absolutely within your reach.

In every moment of every day, you have to decide whether you are going to *create pain* or *create performance*. In any given moment—consciously or not—you are always choosing to create one or the other: chronic stress, anxiety, and being overwhelmed, or resilience, engagement, and opportunity. In each moment, you have to make this choice again, and again, and again—until choosing performance over pain becomes so ingrained that it becomes automatic.

As a leader, this choice is crucially important, because the stakes are much larger than just you and your own world. Whatever you choose for yourself—for better or for worse—is what you will also spread to those who work for you, next to you, and above and below you. Whatever you choose for yourself is also your choice for your organization. The ripple effects are enormous.

IT'S UP TO YOU

What kind of person do you want to be? What kind of leader do you want to be?

I sincerely want for you to be mentally fit. I want you to choose vitality over depletion. To choose opportunity over obstacle. To choose performance over pain. I want you to be that leader whom everyone else wants to follow; the one who shows others through example that there is a different and better reality. My wish for you is to be in alignment with your best self, at work and at home.

Mental fitness is built on choice and skill. Skill can be developed through practice. Choice is just choice. You make the choice, or you don't. If you don't choose to create performance in one particular moment, it's okay, it's not forever. In the very next moment you get another opportunity to choose all over again. You exercise that muscle to choose.

But fundamentally, you have to believe that you do have a choice and that this choice is worth making. If you're still not sure about this, still skeptical, that's absolutely fine! Stay with me. I am confident there's still opportunity to convince you.

Key Points

- It's time to **break the taboo of talking about pain** in a corporate setting.
- Your body's *catabolic* **energy state** is the fight-or-flight response and is destructive to the body. Its *anabolic* **energy state** is healing and restorative, and enables sustained high performance over time.
- **When you perceive a strong threat—real or imagined—it feels the same**, and you become emotionally *triggered*, an extreme catabolic state. Your performance is significantly compromised.
- **Organizations are filled with catabolic leaders** who perform in sub-optimal ways and negatively impact others.
- Executive **pain is very expensive** for organizations in both obvious and hidden ways, causing destructive ripple effects throughout the organization.
- Deep, **sustainable change requires a systemic perspective** and approach.
- **You have the choice**, in every moment, to create pain or to create performance; your choice will affect not only your own well-being but also that of the organization you lead.

4

CREATING PERFORMANCE

Q: Isn't leading lightly too soft to drive results?

A: No, because when you are leading lightly not only are you optimizing your performance, but also you have the added awareness of how to optimize the performance of others.

When you are not triggered, people are attracted to you, inspired by you, look forward to collaborating and working with you. Why? Because you're aware of your impact on others, and you're looking at things far more collaboratively and holistically. You're going to create a much deeper trust in your relationships with others, and things will go faster. When you have trust, it speeds up performance. People aren't second-guessing you. You are going to be more effective in driving results as a result of that, and feeling better the whole time, and modeling this for your team.

Now, sometimes I get pushback from people about this. They say the entire concept of leading lightly is wrong. They tell me: "You need to be tough to create performance." But the people who say this really don't understand the concept of leading lightly. Leading lightly doesn't lower standards. It doesn't lower expectations. It actually increases them, because you can create more clarity about what you are trying to accomplish. You're not softer. You're just coming at it in a way that doesn't create increased anxiety or stress and overwhelm others. But you have the same level of expectations and the same level of standards that you had before. You're just feeling better, and your team is feeling better, and they're more rested as a result of your change to leadership.

It's a myth that you have to be tougher to get results.

We can do better.

That is the inevitable conclusion from what we have talked about up until now. Starting here, we will talk about how to do just that—how it is possible to improve your performance. It begins with you believing that it is possible to improve and then choosing to get better.

There is no one big thing that improves performance. Rather, it is a consistent set of decisions—both big and small—you make literally moment-by-moment, hour-by-hour, day-by-day. Let's examine how that works in practice. I will begin with a story about me, to lay the groundwork. Then you will see what one of my coaching clients—someone I think you may have a lot of common with—did, and we will end this discussion by talking specifically about you.

HOW I DECIDED TO CREATE PERFORMANCE

In the mid-1980s I was a trader on the floor of the Chicago Mercantile Exchange. I was in my early twenties and hell-bent on making good money. I wasn't greedy. I wasn't driven to achieve wealth for social status. Money meant something else to me, something fundamental and deeply rooted in my life experiences.

In the earliest parts of my childhood, I had lived in a warm, comfortable home, embraced by an extended-generation Italian family that was securely anchored by strong and loving grandparents. There was no lack of money, food, or material comforts. But when I was about ten, my grandfather passed away, and my circumstances changed overnight.

For the rest of my youth, I lived in a different city solely with my father in an apartment that felt small and confining. My dad talked about money *constantly*. He worried about money. And he hated the people who—he believed—kept him from getting his fair share. It was always someone's fault that he couldn't get ahead. His perceptional lens (see Chapter 2) was that if you had money, you got it deceptively. You got it through lying, through cheating, through ripping off people, unless, maybe, you were a doctor. He very much had a victim mentality about wealth.

As I mentioned, I was at times malnourished, even while striving to be a top athlete. Throughout the winter, when my father, a union house painter, didn't work much, it was rare for us to have healthy food. And even when he was working, he drank away most of his pay, so there was little money left for food. In this toxic environment of scarcity, fear, and worry, I developed a very particular perceptual lens around money. This lens colored the way I thought about myself and what I would need to do in my life. It went like this:

Having money means having safety. Not having money means vulnerability.

To me, this perception was reality. And what followed was I came to believe that:

- Money is scarce (*safety* is scarce)
- I must never let myself be poor (*unsafe*) again
- The more money I have, the more *safe* I will be
- I must be extremely vigilant and careful with my money (to create safety)

It was with this mindset firmly entrenched that I entered the financial trading world some years later. I was determined to quickly excel (*make money; be safe*), so I studied the other traders around me. I observed that there were two types: There were the guys that had money. There were the guys that did not.

I carefully watched both groups, noting their moods, behaviors, and trading results. They could not have been more different. The guys with money talked about it with excitement and a sense of tremendous opportunity. And they *spent* money. Big risks, big rewards. They were loose, open, and some even cavalier about their finances. They simply expected, without doubt, that they would make more. And that's exactly what they did. Again and again, they made money.

The guys *without* money were the "little guys." They were constantly worried. They were worried about going broke. They counted their pennies. They were worried about market volatility. They looked and acted tight and constricted. Their trades were different, too; they never made bold moves, just tiny trades. I even remember seeing one of these guys in my local neighborhood, after hours, scavenging scrap metal to sell for a few bucks.

As I spoke with traders in both groups and continued to observe them, I came to understand that they had vastly different philosophies, expectations, and concerns. It wasn't a matter of what was objectively true. While the market movements affected everyone, some people were still wildly successful, and others were always just one step away from bankruptcy. And to my dismay, I realized where I fit in. I was one of the little guys. I was always worried about money. Always obsessing about how much I had or didn't have. Always feeling constricted. Always believing I did not have enough.

BOOM! I instantly knew I did not want to be in this group. I wanted to be with the flourishing traders. The people making and spending money; the happy, carefree people. The people whose world seemed to be different from mine.

Then and there, I decided to create the "prototype" of that successful person, the *future me*, so that I could become that person. I chose to adopt a different belief system. I chose to remake myself, to become that person who could authentically believe, "I've got this. No need to worry."

Today, I understand that what I did back then was to make a decision to change my perceptual lens and make permanent changes in my brain's underlying operating system. I taught myself to stop seeing the world through my habitual lens of resource scarcity, and look instead through a new, different lens of resource abundance. The change didn't happen overnight. Rather, it was through a persistent, intentional **practice** that I forced my brain to rewire itself.

Let me give you one example of the actions I took: **I started to give my money away. Every day.**

There were many homeless people around the Chicago Mercantile Exchange. I assigned myself the task of giving away a twenty-dollar bill every time I passed one of them. The first time was excruciating! I thought to myself, "I'm just throwing this money away. This is so incredibly stupid." The whole thing reminded me of my father's bad habit of wasting what little money we had on alcohol.

Still I kept at it. Within weeks I had handed out hundreds of dollars; in today's currency that would be a thousand or more. It was so difficult. I hated myself for giving my money away; I hated it being so hard to do. The whole process was painful. But I kept reminding myself that I had committed to making a change in my beliefs and in myself. I challenged my scarcity lens again and again as I told myself, "You have to believe there is abundance; you have to believe that there is more than enough for you."

After several months, I was surprised to find myself proactively looking for homeless people to give money to. I no longer had any emotional charge to giving the money away. It became an almost automatic response: See a homeless person, give them twenty dollars. It's just what you do.

With this change of perceptual lens, I stopped focusing on what I didn't have. Instead, I focused on what I wanted to have. In the process, I successfully shifted away from worrying about finances and hoarding resources, to feeling and living with abundance. I constantly lived with this new perceptual lens until it became my new reality. Without knowing it, I had changed my underlying operations system. *I had changed my brain.*

Let me give a before and after of how this works in the business world.

PERFORMANCE IS POSSIBLE

A year ago, one of my clients—Joe, an SVP who reports directly to the CEO—arrived for his coaching session clearly upset. He rushed into the room, threw himself into the chair, and in a breathless rush of words immediately started complaining.

Me: Whoa, slow down! What happened?

Joe: The boss asked me for some data he wanted me to dig up. He said it was critical, and even though it was 3:00 PM on a Friday he *had* to have it that night. I had to drop everything! That made me miss a different deadline.

Me: Okay, and . . .

Joe: Everything got messed up. I had to cancel a special dinner with my wife and our friends—something we had been planning for a month. But I worked my butt off to get this done for him. I sent it to him at eight o'clock that night. What a damn joke!

Me: Why? What happened?

Joe: Nothing! Exactly *nothing* happened. That's why I'm so pissed.

Me: Well, what did you *want* to have happen?

Joe: Are you kidding me? The guy should have gotten back to me. Thanked me. Something. Anything! The S.O.B. didn't respond to me for five days. That means he did *not* need this on Friday! That was a lie. Everything is always urgent, urgent, urgent!

Me: So, did you make an effective request? Did you actually ask him to confirm receipt of the data you sent? Or to give you feedback? Did you do anything at all to alert him to the fact that you expected him to respond to you?

Joe: [Says nothing]

Me: And you've been upset about this for *how* many days now?

Joe: Five! Five days!

Me: Joe, listen to me. You've been ranting about this for the past fifteen minutes. And it's five days *after* the fact? This is insane!

Joe: No! You don't get it. This happens all the time with this guy!

Much more often than we think, we are responsible for our own pain.

Me: Yeah, I get it. I get that you think this is about your boss and his crappy behavior. And I get how you think you are being wronged, repeatedly! But there is something else I get, and I want *you* to get it too. I am looking at this from a performance point of view, *your* performance. Look at yourself, and how upset you are and have been for days. Joe, this is not performance. You are hurting yourself now, *and* you are hurting yourself in the long run too. We have to break this cycle. *You* have to break this cycle!

Does Joe's story sound familiar? Do you empathize with Joe? Does someone else (or something else) cause *your* problems? If that other person were to behave differently, or if the situation were different, would you then not be so stressed, overwhelmed, frustrated, or exhausted, or experiencing your pain? But that pain is not momentary. I know you can imagine Joe simmering in resentment for five days, because you have done your version of that too. There have been times you've been stuck in catabolic mood states to your own detriment.

Let's spend a minute on what causes your pain, as the first step toward eliminating it and moving toward performance. I'd like you to pause in your reading and take a moment to reflect on the following. Jot down your answers.

1. When do you get really upset at work, at home, when you are just living your life out in public going to the supermarket, driving to see friends? What triggers you?

2. How long after the trigger do you continue to think about the issue?

3. How about your less intense negative mood states, the frequent
    ones? What do you think causes them? How long do they last?

If you're thinking that Joe's reasons for being so upset for so long are
minor but that *your* reasons are different, *yours* are justified when they occur,
well, hold that thought. I am going to show you how, just like Joe, you
unwittingly engage in your own cycle of pain. And, more important, I am
going to show you how to break that cycle. To do that we are going to use
some incredibly advanced technology—so advanced, it doesn't exist.

It's a type of video camera. In some ways, this "camera" is completely
normal in the way it makes standard audiovisual recordings. It captures all
the usual observable stuff that people say and do. But this special camera
can also detect the thoughts and mood of the people being recorded. So
when we play back the video, we can see thought bubbles above each person's head, and mood bubbles too—indications of their catabolic or anabolic
mood states.

We'll use this unusual camera the way athletes use video to review their
decisions and actions to find the precise moments that contributed to the
win or loss. It's all about feedback and improvement and generating better performance. Our camera will reveal thoughts, moods, behaviors, and
results. Since it's always easier to talk about other people than ourselves, let's
see how the cycle of pain unfolded in the story Joe told me.

#1 "Things Happen" to Joe

Our camera zooms in on Joe sitting at his computer in his office at work. We
see Joe's boss step in. He makes a request to Joe to quickly gather some data
by the end of the day. And we see Joe saying yes, he'll do it.

#2 Joe's Thoughts and Moods Turn Catabolic

We see the boss leave but Joe is still sitting there. But now our camera reveals the thought and mood bubbles around Joe. We see that Joe isn't happy about the boss's request, or more specifically, the *urgent* timing of it. His energy quickly turns catabolic. He becomes angry, frustrated, stressed, and overwhelmed. His mind is reeling. His thoughts come so fast that we can barely read the text in the thought bubbles. *"He always does this! I am going to have to cancel our dinner plans!"* We can see Joe is emotionally triggered.

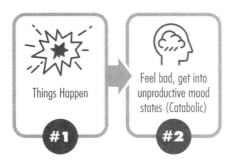

#3 Joe Searches for the External Fix

Over the next few hours, we watch Joe as he works on the assigned task. For the most part, he maintains an outward composure, but we can see what's going on internally. His thought and mood bubbles look like this:

"I can't believe him! He is so unfair."
Mood: Anger

"How the hell will I finish this today? Grab time by skipping the Executive Quarterly Review meeting? Yeah, right..."
Mood: Overwhelmed

"Ridiculous! I'm gonna start looking for a better job. Somewhere that I'm appreciated. If that even exists."
Mood: Doubt

"I'm gonna tell him what I think. I'm gonna tell him that this is not acceptable. No, I'd better not. Probably get fired on the spot."
Mood: Anxiety

Joe is reactive. His thoughts and moods show that is he is unconsciously trying to work the situation: to fix it, change it, take control somehow. And if he can't do that? Well, then he will find a way to avoid this in the future, to prevent it from happening again. Every one of his thought bubbles shows an *external* focus:

- Blaming the unfair boss (a person).
- Worrying about competing priorities (a circumstance).
- Planning a conversation to complain (an event).
- Fantasizing about a new job (people, event, and circumstance all rolled into one!).

Back to our video. Joe assembles the data his boss needed and attaches it in an email and he hits SEND. The clock shows 8:00 PM. Joe puts on his jacket, picks up his work bag, and heads out to go home. But even though

Joe's visible actions are now pretty mundane—he's taking the elevator down, walking to the parking lot, driving home—his thought and mood bubbles haven't stopped. He takes his sour mood with him.

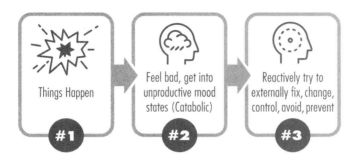

#4 Joe Ruminates

On Joe's drive home, we see him *deliberating* about the whole thing. He thinks about his boss, the request, and his anger about it. It's a loop that won't stop. Joe never figures anything out or comes to a resolution. In fact, we get really bored watching the footage because it is so repetitive.

Joe can't wait to get home, to the comfort of his house, wife, and kids—his sanctuary! But it doesn't help. As he walks in the door, he is still ruminating. Everyone can sense his bad mood, and the kids' initial enthusiasm on seeing him deflates almost immediately.

As we watch the evening unfold, we see Joe throw himself into a chair opposite his wife and launch into his story about his boss. At first, his wife's own thought and mood bubbles show genuine concern for Joe's well-being. But soon, her concern turns into disappointment and sadness, and then into resentment. She doesn't verbalize it, but her thought bubbles show it all: *Again with the boss. So tired of it. Joe just keeps contaminating our home with these ongoing issues. Will it never end?*

Meanwhile, Joe is oblivious to his wife's reactions. He rehashes the story several times. He fails to ask his wife about her own day, or how she is doing, or how the kids did at school. His wife quietly adds that transgression to her private list of growing evidence that their marriage is going south. This is not what she signed up for.

As Joe's rumination goes on for days—five days, in fact—we see him looking increasingly depleted. He seems defeated. His body does not know the difference between the actual situation (which is long over) and the constantly reimagined situation that we see in the thought bubbles. Joe is downright miserable.

Joe goes through these five-day catabolic moods on a regular basis. The results are bad for him, his family, and his organization, as a quick review of what he goes through will make clear.

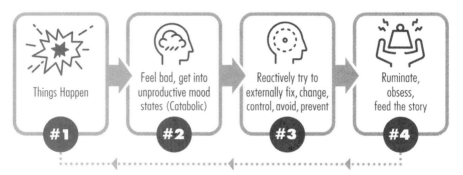

This cycle of pain severely compromises Joe's performance as a leader. He may seem to be holding it all together, but he is not operating anywhere near his potential. Leadership is a complex and demanding role that requires so much more than showing up halfway. The fact is Joe's performance is hurting his team and organization, creating pain that goes beyond his own limited experience. For example:

- As his moods leak, people avoid working with him; he loses key followership.

- He fails to act on his team's concerns and input because he is self-centeredly focused on his own problems.
- He feels stuck, and in his overall inertia he does not pull the trigger on important decisions at work.

It's not hard to see that Joe is sabotaging his chance at future promotions by failing to perform in effective ways. In fact, he may be at risk of losing his current job if he doesn't turn things around. Poor leadership performance is just too expensive for organizations to tolerate for long.

Speaking of the long run: if we were to watch Joe over many years of video footage, we would see this pattern of him creating "dis-ease." In the short run, he feels mental and physical discomfort. But if sustained long enough, Joe will do what many of us do: He will seek temporary escape. He may overuse drugs, alcohol, or food; he may zone out with TV or social media. He'll do anything that's mindless, anything to numb the pain and bring some temporary relief. Of course, this pattern of self-medication and avoidance in turn creates a whole new set of issues. Many years later the cumulative effects of the cycle of pain cause serious physical issues, such as a weakened immune system and increased risk of developing a chronic disease.

MOVING FROM PAIN TO PERFORMANCE

It is more than possible to eliminate the pain Joe (and most likely you) are going through—by creating mental fitness. Before I show you how to do just that, let's see just how powerful the payoff can be. And once again, we will use Joe as an example.

A few months after Joe's incident with his boss, a period of time during which he was working diligently with me to improve his mental fitness, Joe arrived for his coaching session with me in a very different frame of mind. He was relaxed and steady as he thoughtfully reflected on a recent situation.

Mental fitness can eliminate much of your self-inflicted pain.

Joe: [chuckling] So, guess what? Prepare to be "shocked." My boss did it again.
Me: What did he do?
Joe: Oh, you know. The whole Friday night thing. I'm winding down at about 5:30, and he says he wants me to meet with the head of

sales before I leave for my family's weekend trip to Disney. Something about a report—as usual!

Me: How did you handle it?

Joe: Well, right off, I felt that familiar anger start to rise in me. I'm so much more aware of it now. My heart started to beat faster and my shoulders got tense.

Me: Oh, great observations. And in the moment, too!

Joe: Yeah. So, while he was talking, I listened, but I also made sure that I didn't hold my breath, and I even took some deeper breaths to help calm my body down. Like you said, oxygen makes it way easier to think clearly.

Me: That's great!

Joe: Then I realized I was thinking, "Why does he *always* do this to me?" Totally not helpful. So, I switched that up right away and reminded myself that for one thing, I'm not powerless, and for another, he's not *intending* to upset me.

Me: Wow, what a change for you.

Joe: I started asking questions for clarity about his request. Turns out, he had no problem with me meeting up with the sales guy next week, as long as I could get the results to him by Wednesday end of day. He was just concerned I might forget about it if I didn't do it right away.

Me: Why would he make that assumption?

Joe: To be honest, I *have* forgotten things once or twice. Probably because I was so ticked off at the time. But I still have to own it. Anyway, I didn't take it personally. Actually, we were able to laugh about it. He had forgotten something too—the fact that I was going on my family trip! I have to say I'm enjoying him as a person a lot more these days.

Me: When you don't allow yourself to stay triggered, everything feels so much easier and enjoyable.

Joe: It's true. I feel so much lighter most of the time now. Not that much has changed externally, but I guess *I* have changed, so I'm seeing things differently. A few people have even said to me recently that I seem more comfortable, or easygoing, or something. I'm not sure I can explain it. But I do know what they mean.

HOW TO CREATE PERFORMANCE

What a dramatic difference for Joe! He has learned to short-circuit his own cycle of pain and, instead, shift into a high level of performance. He spends more of each day feeling good, in anabolic energy states instead of pervasive catabolic ones. Even though this is a huge difference for Joe, he is no more special or talented than anyone else—no more capable than *you*—in terms of his ability to make that shift. He learned how. He practiced with persistence. He applied it. And if he continues to apply it consistently, this new way will become his new norm. He'll have less and less pain; more and more performance.

This approach is not a magic pill. But my clients' experiences have proven over and over that most people can increase their mental fitness and vastly improve their lives. What happened with Joe is a great example of mental fitness in action.

Let's see exactly what he did—so that you can do it, too.

#1 "Things Happen"

Joe was going along through his day, carrying out his plans. Then, *something happened.* There was a triggering event: Joe's boss came in with a request.

#2 Joe's Thoughts and Moods Turn Catabolic

Next, but almost instantaneously, Joe's *perceptual lens* was activated and he made *an interpretation* that this request was a negative thing that was going to threaten his plans and his time with his kids.

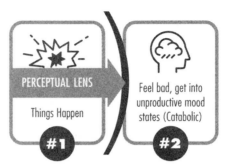

This particular perceptual lens of "danger!" had been shaped early in Joe's life. His father had been an alcoholic, and young Joe had been powerless against his father's drunken rages. When this perceptual lens became activated during Joe's interaction with his boss, Joe's energy rapidly began to shift into a catabolic state with feelings of tension, anger, and dread, caused in part because of the echoes of his childhood.

#3 Joe Quickly Applies Mental Fitness

But Joe did not spiral into rumination. As I said, by the time this conversation occurred, Joe had already been developing his self-awareness and practicing his mental fitness skills for a few months. He was able to notice right away—within seconds—that his mood had started to enter a catabolic state. But he interrupted the cycle of pain. He did not start the usual search for external fixes, or seek to blame others, circumstances, or himself.

Instead, Joe applied mental fitness. He *paused before reacting*. He took measures to calm his body. He noticed his underlying operating system at work: his unproductive thoughts, their familiar pattern, the "default" perceptual lens that was influencing his interpretations. In that very moment, he *challenged these unproductive thoughts*. He remembered that his perspective was just one of the many ways of looking at the situation! He quickly *changed his impeding perceptual lens* to a more *helpful perceptual lens*. This time, he chose a lens of curiosity and empowerment.

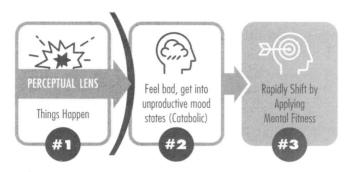

#4 Joe Performs Optimally

With his new and chosen perceptual lens in place, Joe suspended his judgment and sought to learn about his boss's intent and needs. He asked meaningful questions—"What are the sorts of things you are looking for?" and "Can you give me some context?"—and gained more knowledge. He became an active participant in shaping what would happen next. ("Would it be okay if I got this to you after my weekend trip to Disneyland?") As he made this very effective shift, he felt a new sense of relief and capability. His mind no longer perceived a need to fight the enemy or to run away.

As a result, he sensed new possibility and opportunity. His muscles let go of their tension. He became more relaxed and more confident. With this shift into an anabolic energy state, his thoughts, moods, and physiology aligned in such a way that he could now function optimally.

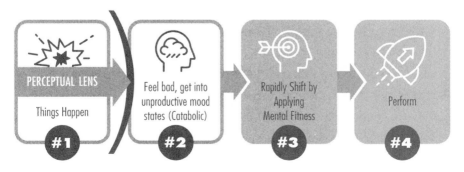

In other words, Joe could now *perform*. He could consciously and deliberately choose what to say and do next, using the full range of his brain's capacity. He could assess his situation more clearly. He generated new, productive ideas for how to proceed—ways that previously he could not have seen or imagined. In a very real way, Joe *created* what would happen next within a positive, productive framework.

And, as he brought this different, positive energy to the situation, he found that his boss also engaged with him differently. They both had the freedom to be lighthearted *and* productive. Instead of draining energy, Joe felt even more positively energized than before the interaction. With this small but important improvement in their relationship, Joe has now set the stage for better future interactions with his boss.

That positive feeling carried over during his drive home, and Joe was really looking forward to seeing his kids. So, when they crashed into him at the door, he hugged them with genuine enthusiasm and listened to their breathless excitement about their upcoming trip to Disney. Joe kissed his wife, noticing that he felt close to her. He asked her about her day, and oh, was there anything he could do to help pack? In fact, there *was* plenty to do, but with the relaxed sense of ease between the two of them, they were able to finish it all up while talking and sharing the details of their respective days.

UNDERSTANDING YOUR HIDDEN OPERATING SYSTEM

Like Joe, you are unknowingly controlled by your own operating system and your perceptual lenses. They're hidden from you. You don't see them for what they are, but they are always running their programs, even in the most ordinary of circumstances. In order to change them, you have to learn to see them. You have to know that they exist and what they are doing

Take a close look at the diagram here. *Don't just skim it,* because it is absolutely critical that you become aware that you have an underlying operating system and that it is always functioning.

The best way to understand your underlying operating system is to think about your computer. The last time you were on your computer, what were you doing? Reading an email? Writing a document? Crunching numbers? Whatever it was, you were using an application. You knew what

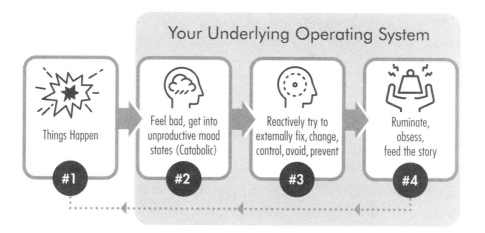

task you wanted to accomplish and you chose the appropriate application to do it.

But here's what you were *not* thinking about: the internal, unseen code that the computer requires in order to run all the different applications that you use every day. In other words, you were not thinking about the computer's underlying operating system, even though it's running all the time under every application that you use. Sure, every once in a while, you think about it when it has a problem, or you have an upgrade to install. But for the most part, the operating system is just there. You don't see it, and you don't think about it.

Your underlying personal, mental operating system works in the same way. It's there; it's in the background; it runs things. And if it is causing you problems and pain, as it was for Joe before he began working on creating mental fitness, it *can be upgraded*. But, that upgrade doesn't happen with one easy click. You'll make your own personal upgrade by leveraging the neuroplasticity of your brain—your brain's capacity to reconfigure itself, to remap the neural pathways that it takes to complete an "application" in your thinking. It takes time, and it requires you to become more self-aware and more skilled, because your brain will resist and will try to default to what it has always known.

How a Walk in the Woods Can Change Your Brain

Imagine we are walking in a lush, grassy meadow. It's a beautiful day—sunny and absolutely glorious! Suddenly, we enter a forest. It's a dark, thick, gnarly woods; it looks like it's been there for eons. We look all around, but all we see is forest. The forest looks scary and difficult. But unfortunately, our car is on the other side of this forest, and we need to get to our car so we can ultimately get home. That means we will have to make the trek through this dense, uninviting woods.

We take our first tentative steps into this dark forest, carefully picking our way, looking for the easiest way to get through. Almost as soon as we enter, something bright catches our eye. About twenty yards to our left, a tiny bit of sunlight streams through the trees. It appears to be an opening in the woods. It's like a beacon, calling to us. We take a closer look, and—yes! There *is* an opening. It's like someone took a giant lawnmower and just mowed right through the intertwined tree trunks, carving out a big, beautiful wide path. Are we going to take it? *Of course we are going to take the easy path.*

And here you have just seen how you unconsciously think.

This story and scenario is about how your brain works. It's about your:

1. Thought patterns
2. Choices
3. Time and effort

Your thought patterns are your automatic ways of responding to things—ways that are typical for *you*. For example, when your spouse says, "Where do you want to go out to dinner?," you may reflexively say, "I don't care. Anywhere you want to go is fine." That's an automatic thought pattern. You don't think about it, you just say or do the thing you always say or do (as does your spouse). Or when you think someone is criticizing you, you respond in your own habitual, defensive way—maybe sarcasm, maybe counterattack, maybe a shutdown.

Your habitual thought patterns are like the lure of that big, open path in the tangled woods. When your brain is confronted with a situation, it quickly and efficiently uses its most well-known pathways. It doesn't want to go through all the effort of carving out a new path. It wants to use the simple, easy, and repeatable process it always has as it sorts through all the information being thrown at it every second.

That's fine in our forest example. We needed a way out, and your brain found it.

But it is *not* fine in situations where our brains have habitually responded in ways that are not helpful to us. Like when we instantly lash out when someone criticizes us for something we have done wrong, or have failed to do. In those situations, too, the brain does what it has always done in the past. ("We are being criticized? Attack!") In those cases, our automatic ways of thinking are not helpful. That means changing your brain will require you to confront this "forest" in a new way every time you are faced with a situation that's challenging or emotionally triggering. *You and your brain will want to take that familiar path.* But that familiar path—your thought pattern—will spiral you into your usual catabolic moods and actions.

As your coach, helping you change your brain, I will be saying to you: Don't do it! *You have a choice.* You don't have to take that path. You can carve a new path—create new thoughts. It is up to you. You will have to *choose* to think and *choose* to experience something *profoundly* different than you have before.

Profoundly different. When is the last time that you thought or felt or experienced something you could honestly say was *profoundly different*? It doesn't happen often.

*There are no shortcuts to changing the way
you react to triggering situations. It requires
mindfulness, situational awareness, and building
emotional intelligence.*

At first, your new thoughts are likely to be fleeting. They will be just barely there. It will take so much effort just to catch them—let alone hold onto them. Initially, they will provide only a glimpse of what you can be. And as you are trying to hold onto this new experience, this new you that is emerging, there will be another part of you that will strongly resist. That part of you is—again—that big, wide, open path. You are drawn to the familiar. Your own internal status quo.

Your brain will do anything to avoid the work of creating a new direction, a new way of thinking and responding. That's why I can't say often enough that *choice* is fundamental to change. It's not about what you *can or can't do*, it's what you will *choose or not choose*.

*Most people are blind to their biases, perspectives,
and prejudices, yet all of these contribute
negatively to what they are experiencing.*

In order to upgrade your operating system—to change your brain and become mentally fit—you have to be willing to create a new path. As you keep doing it, this new path gets wider, clearer, easier to follow. At the same time, that older path—as it's used less and less—will start to fade; the brush and trees grow back and obscure it. This is how the brain's neuroplasticity works. The connections between neurons—the "paths in the forest"—start to change. Old connections fall away, new connections grow. When you choose the new paths consciously and intentionally, you are leveraging your brain's natural capacity for rewiring.

HOW I REWIRED MY BRAIN

I rewired my brain when I changed my mindset from scarcity to abundance. Giving my money to homeless people every day was like me facing the forest. In the beginning, it was such a challenge to refrain from taking the easy, familiar path—to hold onto my money out of fear of scarcity.

The automatic part of my brain told me:

Hey! Keep your hard-earned money. In fact, don't just keep it in your pocket—go save it, invest it, because you never know what's coming down the pike. Remember how bad it was when you didn't have any money? You have to keep yourself safe. No one is going to do that for you. You're all you've got. Money equals safety. Your money equals your safety. Don't jeopardize that.

Besides, what is this homeless person going to do anyway? That's right. He is going to use your *money to buy booze. So, you are hurting yourself and obviously not helping anyone else either. Do not, do not, do not give your money away!*

We have internal conversations like this all the time. At home. Driving to work. At work. After work. At a party. Trying to go to sleep at night. This running internal commentary is *nonstop*. We are mostly unaware of it, but you see how it works to keep us from experiencing something new, from forging through an uncut forest? Look how much internal noise I had to overcome in order to give away a twenty-dollar bill. I had to overcome that same internal dialogue every single day. At any time, I could have given in to that dialogue. But I didn't. Eventually my brain and my whole system got used to the new way, and as I got used to it, I also discovered the merits and benefits and self-liberation of this new way.

I changed my brain. You can too.

START REWIRING YOUR BRAIN

Let's get back now to leadership performance, specifically, *your* performance. What situations, events, and people create stress for you? Please think for a moment, and jot down your answers.

Okay, now, wait! I'll bet you just flew through that, and did not write anything down. Am I right? If so, let me coach you through what has just happened. That was a perfect example of everything we have been talking about. Your brain is so very slippery with how it works! You probably had a fleeting thought, something like this: "Yeah, yeah, I got this, I can just move on." You rationalized that you don't *need* to do it (because you're smart, because you don't have the time, because the answers are obvious anyway, because, because, because . . .).

At a superficial level, this type of thinking is just a set of excuses. But here is what is *really* going on: you don't want the anxiety of having to think about these things.

That's what your brain does. You read or hear new information and you have the *choice* to engage in this new direction, but instead you just want to quickly move on. Stop and sense that impulse for a moment. That's what "flight" feels like. It is an automatic movement to protect yourself from feeling anxiety. So, let's try this again. Make the choice to engage in something that you don't really want to do, and write down what situations, events, and people create stress for you.

Write Your Answers Here

1.

2.

3.

Thank you for that. Next, let's go through a short exercise:

Channeling Your Inner Sherlock Holmes to Improve Your Performance

I'm going to walk you through a brief process. I need you to get into the mindset of thinking like a detective. I want you to be as objective as you can as you consider different facts, situations, and possible patterns. From this perspective, I will ask you to try to find at least one example of a pattern that happens within you at work in your role as a leader.

Here's what you will be searching for: a recurring pattern in which you typically experience an emotional charge that is both negative and lingering (rather than fleeting). Here are some examples of patterns that I find to be common for executives:

- You are frequently annoyed when your team members question your decisions instead of just carrying out what you asked them to do.
- You become predictably angry when you find out that someone did not immediately loop you in on a critical development; you can't believe they didn't tell you.
- You get a familiar sick feeling in your stomach when you have to make a critical decision but you have not been given enough data or time for your analysis.

Do one or more of those examples apply to you? If so, that's fine; however, please don't take the easy way out and skip the effort of thinking through this for yourself! That would be your brain, once again, trying to make you "flee" from change. Try to find your own example by considering the questions here. Remember to think like a detective, using the questions as guidelines. You're looking for (1) a recurring pattern in the context of you as a leader, that (2) is predictably accompanied by you feeling a negative, lingering emotional charge (including being numb or checked out).

Write Your Answers Here

1. What people or relationships at work most irritate or annoy you? Or make you angry?

2. As a leader, when do you feel the most stress?

3. What type of circumstances as a leader do you most dread in your role as a leader? What causes you to lose sleep?

4. When do you tend to "check out"—meaning that you more or less pretend to be present, but your mind is really elsewhere? Or said differently, when do you just feel resigned to whatever is going on?

Okay, so what did you find? I hope you noticed at least two or three patterns. Now consider which of these patterns happens the most often, or which one happens less frequently but is hugely disruptive when it does occur. Pick one of your patterns to work with a little deeper here. Please jot it down as clearly as you can. This pattern is an area where you are not your best self. For some people it is lashing out after someone says something critical about their thinking or performance. In situations like this you are not performing optimally.

How do I know? Because a recurring pattern of negative emotional charges means that your brain is taking the familiar fight-or-flight path. Your whole system is diverting energy and resources to defend itself against a real or imaginary threat. Your attention narrows, you lose perspective, and you are seeing the situation according to what your perceptual lens expects, rather than what the situation may actually be.

IMAGINING WHAT BETTER LOOKS LIKE

What would the same triggering situation be like in a *different* mood state—one that is neutral or even positive? In other words: Imagine the exact same typical annoying or anxiety-producing scenario but this time you *do not have* that familiar negative or numb feeling. What would that be like for you? Can you even begin to sense what that new experience could be?

If you are already building an internal argument against me ("This is ridiculous. How can Jody know about me when she is not there?") then you are, yet again, experiencing your brain's active resistance to change. That resistance has come about because I asked you (your brain) to look away from the familiar path and to imagine a completely new alternative. To your brain, that is a lot of work. *Don't wanna!*

Now if you could choose a different path (even if you can't imagine the details of it yet), how much more effective would you be, as a leader, in that same situation? Think of the better outcomes you could achieve! Can you feel how much energy would no longer be wasted on being irritated, angry, overwhelmed, or anxious—energy that you would now have available to actually deal with the situation? Imagine how other people's experiences of you would be different—better—and how those new experiences would cause new, beneficial ripple effects. It would be good for your personal brand, for future conversations, and for the organization as a whole.

MENTALLY FIT LEADERS IN YOUR WORKPLACE

Take a moment to reflect on the people you have encountered throughout your life. Notice who stands out in a positive way. Over these years, how many mentally fit teachers and leaders have you worked with? If you can think of just a few, that's about right. They're rare.

How do we find this type of leader, these high performers who maintain primarily anabolic energy throughout each day? Not surprisingly, they don't walk around with a neon sign that advertises their mental fitness. In fact, the more that someone has developed mental fitness, the less their ego needs other people to actually know or acknowledge it. They are grounded and solid within themselves.

Mentally fit leaders are extremely powerful creators. They understand that their true leadership power lies within their awareness and their ability to be adaptable and agile in perception and perspective. They know at a deep level that they must be a powerful observer of themselves, other people, and the cultural, political, psychological, and business complexity of any given situation. Because they are present, and observing, when you are with them you are not going to see a lot of visible signs of mental fitness. The tell will be in the quality of your experience with them. You are likely to be your best self when you are around them. That's a natural outcome of mental fitness and anabolic energy. It lifts everyone, creating conditions and relationships that make it easier for everyone to perform at a higher level.

Previously, we looked at characteristics of catabolic leaders. In contrast, here are some of the notable characteristics of mentally fit leaders:

- **They drive results** with sustained commitment and execution. They initiate and move toward what's possible, toward creating something new.
- **They do not deny or avoid reality, or merely focus on the positive.** Whatever needs to be addressed is faced head on.
- They believe that **they have the power or capacity within themselves to impact change.** They are not looking for others to fix things.
- **They own their thoughts, moods, and actions**, including their communications. They take accountability for their failures.
- **They are committed to their own growth** and learning.
- **They don't give in to fear or panic.** They are willing to step into those emotional states and move through them. These states do not impede them.
- **They have a strong sense of self**, an internal compass that guides them. They trust themselves to "do the right thing."
- **They are empathic to others and others' perspectives.** They create followership because they lead with high emotional intelligence and thoughtfulness.
- **They understand what is and is not within their control**, and they respond appropriately. When necessary, they are willing to accept circumstances and reality—"what is."

Let's look at some examples.

Aware Alice

Alice represents the first level of awareness of mental fitness, i.e., the beginning phase. She is aware—"my God, I am always defensive"—but she doesn't know how to change. She lacks the skill.

Aware Alice has more awareness than most people because she's excellent at hearing, understanding, and processing other people's points of view. She is accepting of differences, can evaluate what she hears, and can process it. All that is good, but she can be reactive—defensive, in her case—when confronted with positions that are counter to her own.

Curious Carl

Carl represents the second level of awareness of mental fitness. He is aware and has some correction capacity, but does not always catch the problem at the onset.

Carl does all of what Aware Alice does but adds a dimension. Curious Carl is not extremely attached to his own perspective but is profoundly curious as to how the other arrived at their point of view. He wants more granularity in understanding. Carl's intent is not to pull from what he hears in order to build an argument against it, he actually wants to understand other people's perspectives: "Wow, that is such a different viewpoint than what I was thinking! It is diametrically opposed! How interesting! How did they come to that? What am I missing, I must be missing something. What pieces can I pull in to understand my own view and what I'm not seeing?" He is anything but threatened. Curious Carl is creating, growing, learning, and sometimes changing.

Presence Patty

Parry represents the third level of mental fitness. She not only has the capacity to change, but has changed.

Presence Patty is Teflon. It is rare for her to get threatened and feel triggered. Whatever is in the room—competitive presence, divergent opinions, emotional states all over—Patty can take it all in. She can process and synthesize at a high level. She goes with the flow in the room. She is open and transparent; she is not guarding herself. But she is appropriate too—she has high EQ. Presence Patty can understand what will trigger or threaten each person in the room. She is contemplative about what's good for the organization and team. She is selfless in her own needs. She is not a martyr. Rather she has the perspective that "this is least of your worries, there are bigger fish to fry." She elevates others by what she says, perspectives she shares, and the alignment she creates.

Leaders who perform at the highest level are mature, reflective, and secure. They're not clouded by emotion, reactivity, and ruminating. They're present in the moment. Their mental fitness lays the foundation for optimizing their performance. They have the capacity to handle myriad leadership challenges and conversations that come up moment by moment, both positive and negative. This is a state that minimizes pain for oneself and for other people. It minimizes stress, and it's anchored in resilience—something that we all absolutely need today.

Key Points

- In your role as a leader, **you have one or more recurring patterns** where you predictably feel a negative, lingering emotional charge (including being numb or checked out).
- **The core of what causes you pain is your perceptual lens**, your set of ingrained beliefs about yourself, others, and the world around you.
- **Your capacity to notice when your perceptual lens fails you, and to change the lens, is the key** to your personal and professional transformation in your performance, interpersonal relationships, and life.
- **Mental fitness is all about using choice** and skill to "upgrade" your underlying operating system—including your perceptual lens—ultimately changing unproductive pathways in your brain to create a "new you."
- **When you are faced with an unwanted circumstance or event**, you apply mental fitness to interrupt your spiral of catabolic energy. You pause, change your perceptual lens, and create what happens next within a more empowered, productive framework.
- To "upgrade" your underlying operating system, you will **leverage your brain's neuroplasticity**—its capacity to reconfigure itself.
- **Choice is fundamental, and that choice will be difficult** at first, like hacking a new path through a thick, gnarly forest when you could have just taken the easy and familiar super-highway.
- Most people struggle somewhat at first as their brain resists this "work." **Over time it becomes much easier and the new ways become the new "you."**
- **Developing mental fitness allows you and others around you to have a completely different, better experience.** That will be good for your personal brand, for future conversations and relationships, and for the organization.

5

CHOOSING ACCOUNTABILITY

Q: How do we start to choose accountability?

A: You have to truly believe you are accountable for your thoughts and actions. No blaming. No complaining. No pointing fingers. You have to own it. Accountability is the first muscle you have to work on, because if you don't, you won't really be able to improve. You will (continue to) blame others. You need to increase your awareness of where you are not accountable; where you are slippery and are rationalizing your lack of accountability.

Otherwise, nothing will change.

The ability to choose accountability is your habitual demonstration of:

1. Being responsible for, and having control over your (a) thoughts, (b) moods, (c) behaviors, and (d) outcomes, and

2. The ability to look inward to discern any personal contribution to a situation, rather than reflexively rationalize or blame external factors or others.

I can hear your potential pushback now.

"I am a leader. Obviously, I am accountable. That goes without saying." I've heard some version of that from leader after leader; from mid-level managers to the C-suite; at small businesses and nonprofits all the way to Fortune 10 enterprises. And to be blunt, I don't think it is true. I just don't believe most executives are as accountable as they think.

I have been teaching and coaching accountability for over thirty years—and I have seen that most leaders, initially, are not particularly interested in the topic—unless we're talking about their direct reports! Then they can't wait to tell me about how bad everyone is. Almost no one comes to me truly wanting to talk about their own accountability, because they think there is no need. But within our first hour together in our leadership development workshop series, they are surprised and intrigued as we uncover their specific blind spots around *their* accountability.

Accountability is not a sexy topic, is it? And yet, personal accountability is the absolute foundation of mental fitness. It is completely nonnegotiable. But what, exactly, does accountability mean? Whenever the topic comes up, most of us—just like many of the executives I coach—immediately think about *other* people (not ourselves!), and it's usually in the context of something going wrong.

- "You just can't count on him!"
- "She broke her commitment."
- "I should have known he wouldn't be able to deliver."
- "Leadership doesn't hold anyone accountable; no wonder we have these problems."

Typically, when we say that someone isn't accountable, we mean their behavior, actions, and outcomes are not reliable. We pinpoint what they did or did not do; the result that they did not achieve. I think that definition is a good starting point, but it does not go far enough. My definition is: you are accountable for not only your behavior, actions, and outcomes, but also for your thoughts and your moods.

We could spend all day talking about other people. But this book is about improving *your* mental fitness. *Your* life. *Your* success. What matters is *your* personal accountability. Here's a mantra I would like you to practice, as we begin talking about the first muscle of mental fitness, personal accountability. Say to yourself:

"I am responsible for my:

- THOUGHTS
- MOODS
- BEHAVIORS and
- RESULTS / OUTCOMES."

In this chapter, I will press you to pull your attention away from everything happening externally—with people, circumstances, events—and instead focus on what is going on *inside* of you. The end result we are looking for: You are going to be rigorous with yourself in a new way when it comes to your own accountability. When you develop the personal accountability muscle of mental fitness, you put an end to unproductive, reflexive patterns of thoughts and behaviors such as:

- Blaming others
- Defending yourself
- Procrastinating or avoiding
- Rationalizing and making excuses

Oh, *you* don't do these things? You would never? ("Because they're not professional behavior.") Okay, granted, you may not do them outwardly. You know how to present a professional face; you control what you say and how you act. But inside? Can you really tell me that in your thoughts you never blame, defend, avoid, or rationalize? I know you do, simply because you are human. These are human reactions and they occur in all of us.

*But it's **what you choose to do with them** that matters.*

Personal accountability is a choice. Far more often than you can imagine—moment by moment, aware and unaware—you go through your day making hundreds of choices that either demonstrate personal accountability or do not. You are constantly choosing (or not) to be accountable for all your thoughts, moods, behaviors, and results.

You need to own your thoughts, moods, behavior, and results. What I am calling for is a *radical* level of personal accountability. It starts with the belief that you are the *creator* of all your thoughts, the *creator* of your moods, the creator of your behaviors, and the orchestra leader of your results. If they are constructive, great! If they are all aligned toward success, great again! But if they are not, then you have both the personal choice, and personal responsibility, to change them.

Choice is a decision. A declaration. It is when you say, "this, not that." When you exercise a choice—about anything—you are asserting your unique presence in the world. Every choice is an act of creation. When you make a choice, you demonstrate agency, the will to take responsibility for yourself and for what happens to you. You are telling the world—and yourself—that you live by the belief that you have the capacity to influence or shape your own outcomes in life.

And that you must use that capacity! This is choosing personal accountability.

STRATEGY #1: STOP YOUR STORIES

When was the last time someone—a colleague, friend, spouse, direct report—told you about something that they were upset about? Take a moment to recall what they told you. Then consider the following:

- Who told the story?
- What happened in the story?
- What was the mood of the storyteller? Were they happy? Upset? Confused?
- What was the storyteller's role in the narrative?
- Why did things turn out the way they did—the stated or implied reasons?

Now, I was not there to hear the story. Still, I would bet a whole lot of money that:

- The story was about *something that created difficulty* for the storyteller.
- Whatever that difficulty was, it was said to be *caused by someone else*, or possibly by circumstances or events.
- The storyteller's *mood was catabolic.*
- The *storyteller was blameless* of any wrongdoing, or was the *hero* of the story.

Was I close?

Guess what: We *all* tell these kinds of stories—to other people and ourselves. The stories come from a feeling of pain, anger, disappointment, frustration, or hurt. We want relief, and these stories temporarily accomplish that. We blow off steam. We head off social rejection by proving that we are not the bad guy. We restore some sense of feeling okay about ourselves. We tell these stories to *feel better*. To "win." To be the hero. To look good. There are so many reasons!

STOP TELLING THESE STORIES.

Just stop. Stop telling your stories to other people. Stop telling them to yourself. There is no room for these stories in mental fitness. These stories are the exact opposite of what personal accountability is about. There are many variations, but they are all forms of personal defense mechanisms. They are perceptual lenses that keep you from having to look at, or acknowledge, your part in what happened.

If you had no part, that means you don't have to do anything. (Whew! Not your fault!) Other people need to be fixed or change. Not you! You're just fine.

Below are some examples of what these stories sound like in our thoughts, and samples of the catabolic mood states they generate. Some won't be your style, but I guarantee that at least some of them will resonate. And be sure to take note of that third column; it's what's really going on in your underlying operating system.

WHAT YOU'RE THINKING	WHAT YOU'RE FEELING	WHAT YOU'RE REALLY DOING
That project manager is so difficult. I know I need to talk to her and clear this up. Ugh. Maybe I can get Fred to pass along my comments.	Anxiety, Shame, Numbness	Avoiding
This is totally John's fault. He's all about his own agenda. Always keeping me out of the loop—on purpose!	Anger, Shame	Blaming
Nothing ever changes around here. They just don't care about doing anything the right way!	Anger, Disappointment, Sadness, Hopelessness	Complaining
Really? And just how was I supposed to know about that? All everyone does around here is criticize me!	Indignation, Anger, Shame	Defending
Oh shoot, that report was due today, and I'm not done. Well, it probably doesn't matter if I send it tomorrow.	Anxiety, Shame	Excusing, Rationalizing
I just can't get started writing that business case. I think I'll clear my inbox instead. That would be good to do.	Anxiety, Shame, Numbness	Procrastinating

I refer to these stories—or moves, or habits—as "accountability land mines." When you "step" on one you're trying to protect yourself from making hard choices or doing unpleasant things. You are making sure you don't have to own up to how you have contributed to the situation or outcome.

Can you see that every time you tell these stories, you are practicing the artful dodge of looking away from yourself? It doesn't matter if you say this stuff out loud or not. If these stories are in your thoughts, they lead to compromised performance. It's that simple.

You create and design your life. Period.

So, what is it I want you to do? When you notice yourself engaging in these accountability land mines, I want you to *stop*. If you are in the midst of talking when you notice it, then stop talking. If you are thinking or ruminating, then stop following that line of thought. Instead, acknowledge to yourself—without blame or judgment—that you are out of alignment and you can make a different move. You can choose personal accountability.

STRATEGY #2: OWN YOUR STUFF

There are people who suffer terrible things in life, and their lives are miserable until the end of their days. There are others who suffer the same horrible things, yet somehow, they rebuild their lives in powerful, life-affirming ways. What's the difference? While there can be a lot of factors at play, one of the most powerful elements among the people who thrive is their mindset. They have embraced the thinking of *I can, I must, I will.*

No matter what the challenges: *I can, I must, I will.*

No matter what others say: *I can, I must, I will.*

No matter what seems impossible: *I can, I must, I will.*

This mindset is personal accountability at its very best. It is easy for us to feel inspired by such people. Just think of those who have inspired you—be they athletes, business leaders, political leaders, or artists—and how you admire what they overcame and then achieved.

Conversely, it is easy to identify people who are stuck in a helpless, hopeless mindset. Nothing ever goes right for them; nothing ever works out. No matter what, they can't get ahead, can't catch a break. And nothing is ever their fault. They are quick to tell you all about how someone else—or bad luck, or the unfair system—is causing their troubles. They are resigned, apathetic, depressed. And you find it depressing to be around them. In fact, you probably avoid them, or extricate yourself from their presence, just as soon as you can. They drain your energy.

However, it is not so obvious when *your* own mindset has flavors of victimhood. Victim mentality is not an all-or-nothing lens. It is entirely possible for you to have a victim mentality about some things but not others, or in particular circumstances only. But it is victimhood nonetheless, situational as it may seem, and it hinders your well-being, performance, and overall success.

Take a look at some examples of victim-mentality thoughts and moods that might occur in the workplace. Notice, too, the third column with the hidden, underlying core thought.

Are you connecting with what I'm saying here? If not (or even if you are to some degree), notice any resistance you have. Listen to your inner dialogue. In how many ways are you rationalizing that much of this does not apply to you?

Note that I am not saying you *are* a victim, or that you think of yourself as such. But is that what you are hearing or interpreting? I am talking about a particular perceptual lens, the victim's lens. But the lens is not you. It's just a perspective that you hold at times.

Think of the last time you felt like something was unfair to you. Now, maybe it really *was* unfair—that does happen in life. And maybe it was unusual for you that you felt that way. But ask yourself, honestly, how familiar is this feeling for you? Before you go on to the next question, pause. Make sure you really thought through this question. You will have a chance to write down your answer in a second.

Now, think of the last time you felt like you weren't good enough, capable enough, or could not achieve something. Again: how familiar is this feeling?

WHAT YOU'RE THINKING	WHAT YOU'RE FEELING	YOUR UNDERLYING CORE VICTIM THOUGHT
You go out on a limb, and for what? They do what they want anyway. Why even bother?	Disappointment, Resignation	"It's hopeless."
This **workload** is so unfair. I'll never **be** able to get it **all** done.	Overwhelmed, Stressed	"I can't."
I don't trust him; I don't trust any of them. I just know they are up to something. Gotta watch my back.	Fear, Distrust	"I am not safe."
I never should have said that. I screwed it up again. Like always.	Disappointment, Anxiety, Regret, Depression	"I can't. I'm not good enough."
This sucks! Why do I always have such bad luck? Life is so difficult.	Anger, Disappointment, Hopeless	"Woe is me."
Why is she such a superstar? I never get any credit around here. It's not fair.	Envy	"Poor me."
I just wish that I didn't have these anxious thoughts. I just wish I could control my mind. But I just can't.	Anxiety, Hopelessness	"I can't."
It's easy for you to say! You're not in my shoes. You don't know what it's like for me.	Anger, Resentment, Hopelessness, Overwhelmed	"It's not fair. Poor me."

Finally, think of the last time you thought that someone was actively working against you, actively trying to make things difficult for you. How familiar is this feeling?

Assess Your Victim Mentality

1. When was the last time that something unfair happened to you?

2. What was the last time you felt that you couldn't, or you weren't good enough?

3. What was the last time that someone was actively working against you?

You probably feel like a victim some of the time. So, how quickly could you think of the examples above? If any of them came quickly and easily, then that tells me that at least some of the time you employ a perceptual lens of victim mentality. That's probably true even if there was only a little bit of familiarity for you.

The good news is that with awareness, you now have the opportunity to let that lens go.

Choose the lens of personal accountability instead.

With this lens, you will not see yourself as a victim. Sure, you may acknowledge difficult circumstances, and that you feel confused or anxious or unsure of how to proceed at times. But when you find yourself in those situations, what you do next is to *quickly* determine what you have control over and what you don't. Even if there is absolutely nothing you can do about the circumstances, you recognize that you always have a choice and control over your thoughts and moods. So that's where you place your attention. You own the (temporary) victim mentality and you change it for the better. Change it to what? You'll hear more on that in the next chapter when we talk about the muscle to choose a helpful perceptual lens.

STRATEGY #3: BE IMPECCABLE WITH YOUR PROMISES

Have you made the connection yet between personal accountability and your effectiveness as a leader? Whatever you do—however you behave—sets the tone for those around you. People will do as you *do*—not necessarily as you *say*—for better or for worse.

Over time, employees will self-select in (or out) of your organization according to their willingness to operate as you do. Your corporate culture— formed by you and the other leaders—is maintained by the concentration of "opted-in" people who are thinking, feeling, and behaving in a similar manner as their leadership. As a leader, you *must* embody personal accountability at all times. It must be strongly evident in your personal brand. If it isn't, then you cannot expect anyone else to demonstrate accountability. Why would they?

Each time you exhibit a behavior that undermines accountability, such as the land mines we discussed earlier, you are showing others exactly how to do that, too. You are actually *teaching* your entire organization how to practice the enemies of accountability! That's not what you are paid to do.

One very effective strategy to embody accountability is to become impeccable with the way you make, manage, and keep promises. We're going to look at that now. However, we won't just focus on the observable part of keeping a promise; we're going to become very interested in the thoughts and moods that lead us to keep or break them.

Please examine the following example. It is so simple, yet it happens all the time.

> While at a conference, Victor, a vice president of technology, was introduced to Maria, who happened to be a manager of one of Victor's clients. Maria told him about her company's upcoming technology implementation, a major effort that was well into the planning stages. As the conversation went on, Maria and Victor identified a mutually beneficial opportunity for Victor's company to get involved in the implementation. Victor told Maria he would be in touch after the conference.

> Later, Victor spoke with his colleague Alexis, who was also at the conference. If anything was going to happen with Maria's company, Alexis would become a key player.

Victor: "I've never met Maria before, but she seemed really interested in integrating our ordering system into their new enterprise application."

Alexis: "That's really promising. So how were things left? Is there a next step?"

Victor: "Yes, I am going to email Maria tomorrow when we get back to the office."

Alexis: "Great! Please copy me when you do."

Victor: "Yes! Will do."

Pretty simple promise, right? But here is how things actually played out.

Victor forgot to follow up, but then remembered a few days later. "Maria's integration is still in the planning stage," he said to himself. "It won't be that big of a deal if I email her next week instead of right now." He rationalized that his procrastination was fine, because the consequences of not keeping the original promise seemed minimal to him. It would be "okay" to let personal accountability slide this time. Victor made a note in his calendar about contacting Maria the following week, but he didn't say anything to

Alexis about any of it. "No need to highlight my bad memory," he thought. "She probably won't even notice."

But Alexis did notice. She had been watching for that email with each passing day. She thought to herself: "We need this integration to happen. Maria's company is a huge client! Victor has always seemed a bit flaky to me. I always wondered about him. Now this. It's more than being flaky. He's actually *unreliable*. Now I have to spend my time and energy to make sure we don't leave Maria hanging. I would hate for her to think we aren't serious about this!"

Usually, the story would end here, with Alexis pondering how to handle the situation. But as it happens, Victor was being coached by a MindMastery® Certified Coach™ around personal accountability. So, when he reflected on this situation for a few days, he shared his analysis with me:

"I broke my promise to Alexis, so I'm going to follow up with her and apologize. I'm also going to follow up with Maria today. I need to close the loop on the vague commitment I made at the conference. I realize now that I tend to think of my promises as 'flexible.' But I need to follow through with all of them, regardless of whether I personally think that the consequences are large or small. Even when I'm going to fail to deliver on a 'small' promise, I need to proactively inform those affected.

"I'm glad that Alexis was honest with me about her irritation. It wasn't what I'd wanted to hear. But, I learned that in her eyes, my reputation and credibility took a big hit. Even more, the damage extended far beyond this one incident."

Notice Victor's thoughts that led him not to keep his promises. What are *your* thoughts when you don't do something you said you would? Any time you make an offer to do something, or say yes to a request, you are actually making a promise. But perhaps you—like many of us—don't think of it that way. What you say to others is more of a "maybe." Something flexible.

An idea. An indication. A loosely held intention. None of those ways of thinking reflect personal accountability.

Three Kinds of Promises

There are three kinds of promises (i.e., making an offer to do something, or saying yes to a request). When you make a **strong promise**, you have every intention of keeping it. There is no doubt you are going to do what you said you would. You know in your bones that the other person can count on you. Someone at work needs your help and asks, "Can you get that to me by Friday?" You are going to help them out. You are going to deliver before the end of the day Friday.

When you make a **shallow promise**, it will sound to others exactly like you are making a strong promise, that your yes is absolute: "Yes, you will get it to them by Friday." But your thoughts tell a different story. You think: "I am going to keep this promise . . . unless Jim doesn't come to me with that other stuff. Because if that goes down, that's going to take priority. But, hey, we don't know yet if that is going to happen. I won't worry about that now. But if that happens, there is no way I can help." Mentally, you reserve a private out for yourself, because you were never committed to the promise (in spite of what you said).

A **criminal promise** will also sound like a strong promise. But you have absolutely no intention of keeping this promise—and you know that at the time of making it. You are just saying the words and going through the motions. "Yeah, I will say yes, because it is easier than dealing with the blow-back of saying no. And who knows? Maybe I will have some time, but I doubt it. Besides, she is always inventing fake deadlines, so I probably have a few more days."

It's amazing how we can rationalize shallow and criminal promises. If you are going to embody personal accountability, you have got to stop making them. Whether you intend to break your promises or "it just happens" through your lack of attention, doing so will ultimately destroy others' trust in you and ruin your personal brand.

When Something Goes Wrong

All that said, there will be times that you will break a promise or commitment. Things will happen that are out of your control and make it impossible for you to keep your promise. Or perhaps you misunderstand something, or you make a mistake. Whatever the reason, your broken promise is likely to have negative impact on others. You inadvertently create breakdowns for them.

When this happens—and it does, with all of us—you should proactively address it by making an effective apology, which is composed of four separate elements:

Part 1: State what you failed to do and apologize to everyone involved. Take full responsibility for not managing and keeping the promise.

Part 2: Acknowledge the breakdowns you must have caused for others.

Part 3: Ask what actions can be taken to repair the damage done.

Part 4: Make a new promise, if appropriate.

Since Victor broke his promise to Alexis, here is what an effective apology from him might sound like:

Part 1: "Alexis, I need to apologize to you. I said I would get in touch with Maria right after the conference, but I didn't. I dropped the ball."

Part 2: "I understand that I could be jeopardizing this unique opportunity if Maria decides that we are disorganized or not fully committed."

Part 3: "I am not sure what I can do to restore your willingness to count on me. I hope that my honesty in this conversation is a new start."

Part 4: "As far as Maria is concerned, I promise, truly this time, that I will email her by the end of day today and copy you."

This is another way of being accountable.

STRATEGY #4: STOP RESCUING AND ENABLING

The most difficult blind spots to see in ourselves are those that drive seemingly—and that is the key word here, *seemingly*—"good" or "positive" behaviors. When we are engaged in catabolic thoughts, moods, and behaviors, and someone brings that to our awareness, we can more easily see that they are not productive. But what about when we think we are doing something good? Helping someone? Being generous? Being supportive?

One of the hidden enemies of accountability is *rescuing* or saving others. Typically, when we do this, we see ourselves as being helpful, and we believe that our motive is positive and generous. That's not to say we cannot or should not ever assist anyone. However, some of us have a *pattern* of frequently and reflexively jumping into situations to "help." Or even be the hero. This behavior shows a blind spot that on some level we are personally invested in being perceived by others as helpful. People with this pattern powerfully resist seeing this blind spot because they believe they are simply being good people and doing the right things for others.

What exactly are we talking about? Helping is more likely to be rescuing or enabling when any of the following occur:

- You *repeatedly* do the same actions for the same person or in the same situation; it's recurring. For example, you have a direct report who you really like, but they are not capable as they should be, so you do some of their work for them.
- You feel *good about yourself* for having been able to help, save, or rescue someone and doing so has become a habit for them.
- Because of your help, the person receiving the assistance was able to *avoid* their own personal accountability in the situation.

If you engage in rescuing or enabling, please recognize this behavior is *your particular form of avoidance*. For one thing, **you are** keeping your focus away from yourself and away from your own development—as in "I'm fine, let me help you instead." And for another, you are avoiding having the difficult conversation with the other person about their own lack of accountability, i.e., their need to improve.

This type of avoidant behavior is rampant among some leaders. Leaders have many inner motivations for enabling their poor performers:

- **Don't wanna.** They don't want the discomfort of performance management or firing someone.
- **Looking bad.** They don't want to admit that they made a bad hire or that their unit has been producing substandard work.

- **Pleasing others.** They want to be liked by everyone; they feel really good about themselves when someone seeks their help.
- **Care-taking.** They are simply nice and don't want to hurt anyone's feelings.
- **Insecurity.** They have anxiety about not being good enough, so they bolster a (false) sense of superiority by keeping or hiring weak talent.

In every case, the leader is not thinking about the longer-term consequences of their rescuing behaviors. Nor are they conscious of what they are actually doing: finding ways to head off their own anxiety or discomfort that they believe would arise if they were to deal with the situations in a more direct manner. They are using avoidance to soothe themselves, to quell feelings that they do not want to experience.

Blind spots around avoidance are very hard to detect. If you tend to be a helper, here is what you can do:

1. Notice the impulse to help, and pause before you jump in.
2. Look through the lens of personal accountability. Has the person you are about to help already taken full accountability themselves?
3. If not, consider having a conversation about that instead of simply rescuing the person. If you are their leader, that conversation is absolutely appropriate.

Be prepared to work through your own discomfort, too. By not rescuing or enabling, you are making a different choice than usual, and that can feel hard at first.

Hang in there! You are embodying personal accountability. You are demonstrating to yourself and others a different way of being. But beware, there are potential road bumps that can pop up along the way.

POTENTIAL ROAD BUMP #1: YOU LACK AWARENESS

You may feel that I use strong language when I talk about accountability. You're right. I do. I am passionate about it, passionate about the dramatic difference it makes. The strong language is not intended to make you feel bad. What I want you to recognize is that lack of accountability is just a habit. *It is not who you are.* It's how you approach situations.

I use the strong language and emotion to try to break through your defenses, to shake you up. Not so you feel bad, but so that you can see. So that you become *aware.* Your part in this is to check in with yourself—observe yourself with a detective lens—as often as you can.

At first you will probably be unaware in the moment. You will not see yourself in action. However, you can reflect later. Ask yourself some simple questions: Did I blame someone or something? Did I justify, make excuses, or rationalize? Did I avoid someone, something, or myself? We all do these things. We come to this honestly, and we are unaware we are doing it. It is not an accident that we have blind spots. Our egos do whatever is necessary to make us feel okay about ourselves. There is a powerful drive to remain unaware.

Remember too that all the muscles work together and support each other. Later on we will explore a different muscle—the muscle of self-awareness—in great depth. Everything that you learn there will help you increase your awareness around your personal accountability.

POTENTIAL ROAD BUMP #2: YOU'RE NOT BUYING INTO THIS

Sometimes people are skeptical of the idea of radical personal accountability, or simply remain unconvinced. If *you* have any lingering questions or doubts, read the four questions I get most often about this.

"Who can control their thoughts? My thoughts just come into my head whether I want them or not!"

Thoughts arise, but you can train yourself to manage them. I am not saying you will stop having certain thoughts. Your brain produces thoughts—that's what it was built to do. However, you can learn to allow your thoughts to pass without creating any emotional impact or response in you. You observe them, but you do not react or respond. The thought—not the event—is what creates the response and the reactivity; it's not the event itself. So, you need to understand your predilection for thinking a certain way. Otherwise you are going to have a very similar response whenever a particular scenario comes up. If this seems far-fetched to you right now, please know that brain training is a process, something that you practice and develop—just like anything else. I will be showing you how.

"I work in a toxic environment. That's what causes my negativity."

There is a lot of toxicity around us, and this is one reason why we need to develop mental fitness. But to your point: First, the toxic environment does not *create* your moods. You have thoughts that arise in response to your toxic environment, and you react to these thoughts. That's what creates your negative moods. In fact, you can work in a toxic environment and become like Teflon. You can embody "non-reaction," and curiosity, both of which help to mitigate the toxic environment.

In addition, and perhaps more powerfully, you can choose to leave that environment and work in a higher-functioning place. If you stick to your story that your toxic workplace is causing your bad moods—and you continue to stay where you are—you are simply practicing the habits of blame and avoidance.

"What if I am innocently driving my car, following all the rules, and some idiot hits me? How am I accountable for that?"

This is a great question. Unfortunately, you were at the time and place that the incident occurred. You didn't cause it; you were just occupying the space and time of the event. The event simply occurred and you were part of it. In that sense, you might say that you were a victim.

You can't change events or circumstances. But in terms of personal accountability, the question is what *can* you control. The answer, you can control your perceptual lens; your thoughts and moods. The typical response would be to perceive this incident as negative. In actuality, from an objective standpoint, it is neutral. It is just something that happened. The most helpful lens you can adopt is the recognition that you don't actually know *what will evolve* from this incident. There can be positive as well as negative impacts. Let me give you an example.

I was driving down a narrow Chicago street across from a high school. All of a sudden, I saw a car heading toward me. The driver was a kid who barely seemed old enough to drive. He was not watching the road. He was not watching my car. He was looking off to the side, his eyes absolutely glued to an attractive classmate walking nearby. In that moment I thought, "OMG, we are going to crash head-on!"

Which we did.

I saw the whole accident unfolding, but there was nothing I could do to avoid it. I could clearly see the boy's face. At the moment of impact, he was completely shocked. In that instant, I could see that he was a new, inexperienced driver; that he had never been in an accident; that he was absolutely terrified of what was going to happen next.

Once I saw that no one was hurt, I got out of my car and walked over to him, and I started laughing. I said, "Dude, are you serious? She's way out of your league! Wait! It's a great story! Do you think you could get a date out of it?"

He looked at me, astonished. I continued with a smile, "Tell me, was she really worth the accident?" He started laughing too and said no. And then we did the whole insurance thing, exchanging information, and I told him to keep his eyes on the road in the future.

I wasn't angry. When there is a car accident, you think of many negative impacts. Upset, injury, expense, inconvenience. Sure, in the very first moment that I realized my car had been hit, I was annoyed as all of those impacts flowed through my mind. But as I looked at the kid, distraught as he was, I knew that it wasn't going to serve me or him to go over and ream him. As it was, he was going to get it from his parents and take a hit to his insurance. In one second, I made the decision that I had to lighten it all up. And honestly, in that moment it really was very funny to me.

I tell this story because when an incident or situation occurs, there are actually many possible responses. There are the typical ones, but some responses can be completely out of the ordinary. Yes, I have been in other accidents and I have been upset in the "typical" manner. But in this case with this kid, I had presence of mind to apply something else, to take a different approach.

When any incident or situation occurs, we usually assign an evaluative "good" or "bad" label to it. But things don't always turn out the way we initially think. Something seemingly positive can have disastrous results later. For example, when a young entertainer finds sudden success and becomes a celebrity—but is not prepared for the changes and pressures this brings. That can lead to stress, illness, or even suicide. Similarly, when people win the lottery, they often end up with more debt and problems than they had before they won.

On the other hand, seemingly terrible incidents can become catalysts for dramatic positive growth and change. People often report that a loss of their job leads to a new, better job and company. People who view a life-changing illness through a lens of personal growth usually report that the illness turned out to be a blessing in disguise—if not the greatest blessing of their life.

When difficult things happen, the lens of personal accountability reminds us that regardless of the external impacts, we are still in control of our reactions to them. In other words, we have a choice.

"It seems like you are blaming the victim. There are a lot of suffering people all over the world. You're saying they all caused their own poverty, their own misery?"

Mindset is *one* of the core factors, not the *only* factor, in determining what we can make happen. The people I work with have sufficient resources to live. They are not in survival mode. When my students or clients want to engage in the world-poverty argument, it is usually an intellectually expressed form of their own avoidance. The unconscious move is "Let's talk about starving people on other continents so we don't have to talk about *me*." Certainly, there is a philosophical conversation that can be had—and a deep one at that. But there is a time and place for that inquiry. If you are seeking to develop your own mental fitness, keep your focus on *you*.

Key Points

- The first step in taking personal accountability is to **stop telling stories** to explain away why something went wrong (or to put yourself in the best light).
- Face reality head-on. **Own your situation.**
- Personal accountability means, among other things, **you keep your promises.**
- **If you break a promise,** or otherwise do something wrong, **apologize.**

  Apologizing is a five-step process: State what you failed to do and apologize to everyone involved; take full responsibility; acknowledge the breakdowns you must have caused for others; ask what actions can be taken to repair the damage that was done; and make a new promise, if appropriate.
- **Stop enabling and rescuing those** who need to take accountability of their own.

6

SELECTING A HELPFUL PERCEPTIONAL LENS

Q: Can I really be successful when leading lightly means accepting difficult situations?

A: Yes, because leading lightly is the result of several choices you make. And the first must be that leading lightly is possible, even under even under conditions that we would normally label as stressful or difficult. That can be a challenging choice for people who feel that this lens means (or signals to others) they aren't taking the problem or situation seriously—that they are irresponsible or a Pollyanna. (Many people have never experienced anything approaching relative ease in the midst of challenge, so it can seem totally Pollyannaish to them.) They fear they cannot solve a problem if they are not "intense" about it.

There is a second subtle, but important, choice you have to make going in. When you face a difficult situation, choose the lens of acceptance to begin. Sometimes things are just hard—but when we accept that and stop fighting or resisting that fact, at least we aren't adding in more difficulty and stress than is already inherent. Acceptance is not resignation. Resignation is a catabolic state—one of hopelessness, lethargy, and the inability to move. There are times when accepting "what is" is the fastest way out of pain. For example, suppose you get fired. You could go through a lot of emotional states over the loss, but the quicker you move to acceptance, the quicker you can move forward and do something about it.

Here's a process that will help you select a more helpful lens:

1. Consider recurring situations that you immediately label as *difficult* or *stressful* whenever they occur.
2. How does that label affect your mood in that moment?
3. How does that label and mood then affect, or drive, your subsequent approach to the situation?
4. Consider whether you are willing to loosen that label.
5. Explore any resistance that you may have to the idea that while the situation may be "unwanted" or have some real-world challenges, you yourself don't have to be as highly stressed as you've always been in the past with this situation.
6. Then come up with a new thought or belief that you're willing to try out. Play with the wording until something feels like an acceptable stretch to you.

> *You want to learn to identify deeply held perspectives that are impeding you and replace them with perspectives that support you and help you thrive.*

When I started out as a runner—the person who delivers orders to buy and sell—on the floor of the Chicago Mercantile, I had an extraordinary belief in myself and what I could accomplish, even though the odds were against me. I was one of a handful of women working there and I was an industry outsider at that. But my perceptual lens—how I saw the world—was one of *possibility*. Even if I didn't know yet how I was going to achieve my goals of financial and professional success, I believed I *would* achieve them. I trusted—and believed in—my own innate capacity.

The environment in which I found myself on the trading floor was brutally difficult. When you are a beginner there, no one helps you. No training programs are provided—at least not at the firm where I started. It's a frenetic atmosphere. You're just thrown in, drinking from a fire hose of chaos all around. It's survival of the fittest. And there is always the risk that you will make a very expensive mistake. The whole experience was like being dropped into the middle of a foreign country where you don't speak the language, and few of the locals are friendly. Check out the newbie—she won't last long! *Ha ha, typical rookie mistake!*

It really was another universe, especially for a woman, in an aggressively competitive, male-dominated world.

My First Day on the Job: What It Can Teach You

While eventually I worked my way up to trader, I entered the business working part-time at minimum wage as a runner for a company called Clayton Commodities. My manager was a gruff old guy. The first time I met him was on my first day. After we introduced ourselves, he asked, "Do you drink?"

I said, "No."

"Do you smoke?"

"No."

"Do you swear?"

"No."

"You will."

With that said, he abruptly walked away.

Now, I want you to imagine, during the first five minutes of walking into your new job, what's your reaction to this conversation? Shock? Destabilizing? Poignant? Funny? It was all those things—and it had my head spinning. And it wasn't an isolated conversation. It was one of many conversations and events that took place that were way outside the norms of a typical company.

continued

I can't think of another place where someone is thrown into a workplace environment that has a self-contained culture, where thousands of people work under one roof for hundreds of different companies who do business together.

There were new experiences, new norms, new beliefs, new financial instruments, and new financial data thrown at you constantly. It was an environment that forced you into adaptability, agility, and a heightened awareness of yourself and your environment. And, it was also a great petri dish for challenging your beliefs, your values, and your understanding of how the world works.

The workplace shapes all of us.

Your industry. Your workplace. The culture of your company. All these components will shape you in ways that are both conscious and not. While all these environmental factors are influencing and shaping your perceptual lens—how you see the world—you ultimately have the opportunity to choose the beliefs, the values, the attitudes, and the perspectives that will serve you best. Those choices, particularly your beliefs, will ultimately shape your life experience, and what's possible or not possible for you.

But my perceptual lens was anchored in the assumption of *opportunity*. I thought: Look at this. All around me there are six or seven thousand successful men doing this exciting work, and having the potential to make a lot of money. They are not stuck at a desk. They aren't slaves to the clock or dealing with corporate bureaucracy and red tape. They are right here. And you are right here. Jody, use this opportunity!

So, I became very strategic. I wanted to identify the big guys, the ones who really made it. I started asking around, "Who are the most successful traders here?" Once I figured that out, I went up to each of them casually and asked, "If you could work anywhere, for any company, what company would that be?"

"Goldman Sachs is *the* place to go," just about everyone told me. Many also added, "But don't bother, *you* won't get in. It is incredibly hard to get hired."

PICTURING—AND PRACTICING—SUCCESS

One day, just after I left the building for the day, I thought I'd forgotten something out on the trading floor. I went back in. No one was there except the janitors who were sweeping up all the trading cards scattered everywhere. I noticed a rumpled coat on the floor in the corner, thrown there by some careless trader. It wasn't just any old coat; it was a coveted RED coat. My own yellow coat signified that I was a low-level worker bee. But the red coats? They were worn by the people who had really made it: the traders.

Opportunity. I knew what I needed to do. I stole the coat. (Don't worry, the coats were rentals and people lost them all the time. No one got penalized.) I took it home. Washed it. Pressed it. Then I assembled the rest of the necessary props to make myself into a (pretend) trader. I had some used trading cards I had gathered from the trading floor, and I made myself a badge. Instead of names, all the traders used acronyms. So I did too, selecting one that I really liked—SOAR.

Every night at home after work, I used my imagination to visualize and practice trading. I would stand up and imagine trades, yell to buy or sell commodity contracts and write on my cards, as if I were on the actual trading floor. It was all pretending, all acting. But I believed in myself as I practiced. Over and over, I truly saw myself as a trader, making money, living in abundance. I imagined myself as having already achieved my goals.

After three and a half months, I accomplished the very thing that I was told would never happen: I was hired by Goldman Sachs as a futures arbitrage clerk. So far, so good! True, I wasn't (yet) a trader, but now I was part of the world's best financial services firm.

As soon as I started at Goldman, I began working toward my next objective. I asked the most successful traders: "For someone who is really talented, ambitious, and aggressive, what is a reasonable amount of time to expect to become a trader here?" I was told it was about three years. That became my next goal: "I will move from arbitrage clerk to trader within three years."

About six months shy of my third anniversary at Goldman, I made an appointment to speak to the president, John Gilmore. People at my level just didn't do that—go see the president. My intention was to find out the likelihood of becoming a trader within the next six months. As I sat in front of John, breathlessly awaiting his answer, he chewed on his cigar and smiled.

"Jody, relax. We love you. There is no doubt that you *will* be a trader here. We absolutely see your potential and believe in you. But, Jody, please understand. People advance here in a strictly hierarchical manner. For a slot to open up for you or anyone else, some other trader has to be promoted first or a need has to arise for additional traders. You won't be called up in the timeframe that you want. But you're slated to be a trader. And, your best chance to be a trader is right here at Goldman Sachs. No company will hire you to be a trader if you're not *already* a trader. It's just not a position that people get hired into. In my estimation, it will probably be a couple of years before you're promoted. Be patient. Put in your time. It's going to pay off."

I thanked John for the information and (politely) pushed back. I said, "I *will* have my badge on or before my three-year anniversary. It's going to be here at Goldman Sachs, or it's going to be somewhere else. I want it to be here. But one way or the other, it *is* going to happen. I just wanted to give you the courtesy of knowing that if you want to keep me at Goldman, you'll need to give me a badge in the next six months. Otherwise, I'll need to look elsewhere."

I *chose* not to believe what he told me. I had *zero* doubt that I would have a badge on or before my three-year anniversary. As the next few months passed, I focused on getting that badge. I was driven by the belief that not only was it *possible*, it was *going* to happen.

And it did—on the exact anniversary of my third year of getting hired. But it was not at Goldman Sachs; I accepted an offer from another well-respected company, Kidder Peabody. John was not happy to see me leave and complained about the short notice that I gave him. But years later, I learned directly from him that he was actually delighted by my audacity, and often told the story of my conviction and drive.

Based on my personal and professional background, who was I to believe

I could do all of this? There was nothing about the way I grew up that told me I could be this successful. In fact, just the opposite. Growing up, I had been made to feel even less than unacceptable—inadequate would be more accurate—because my father and I were poor.

My father lacked any self-awareness, other awareness, or capacity to ever cheer me on as I grew up, or to instill in me a sense of positive self-esteem. In fact, he created an atmosphere of fear, anxiety, and insecurity. It wasn't his intention, but it was his lens, his own upbringing, that created the catabolic environment in which I grew up. In fact, I remember overhearing my father telling my grandparents when I was in the eighth grade, "It's too bad Jody won't go to college. She will just have to go to work. I sure as hell don't have money to pay for college."

Even then, I rejected this forecast. I said to myself, *If that's how it is, then I will have to save and pay for college myself.* There was no way that I was going to let my upbringing determine my future. I was clear that if I was going to make it in life, it was going to be because of *me*. My father's misery was not going to be my path. I made the choice to discard the "truths" I'd been taught and instead *chose* what I wanted to believe about myself—what I wanted my lens to be. I did so without any evidence or proof. And then I lived according to my deliberately chosen perceptual lens.

It wasn't just the lens that resulted in my success; it was the whole integrated chain of alignment among my beliefs, thoughts, moods, and behaviors—all of which I worked extremely hard to create. I didn't have people modeling positive, constructive behavior as I grew up, and I was aware of that, even very early on. I remember thinking when I was about six, "I am in trouble. I have a mom who is really sick. She's here and then she's not here. I have a dad who acts bad. He drinks and sometimes he just doesn't go to work." And yet, I knew that even then, "I need to grow myself up." I remember watching all the "wholesome" family sitcoms at the time, shows like *Leave It to Beaver*, which showed how successful suburban families lived day-to-day to try to understand how people are supposed to behave.

I told you that story so that you can do the same thing that I did, only faster and more efficiently. Over time, as you become aware of your own core beliefs and assumptions—or perceptual lenses—I want you to be very analytical about them. Get into a habit of challenging them. Use this framework:

- Is this lens **impeding** or **helpful**?
- Was this lens **indoctrinated** into me or **deliberately chosen**?

To increase your mental fitness, you will need to replace *indoctrinated, impeding* perceptual lenses with *deliberately chosen, helpful* lenses. Working with your lenses is not a linear process. In many ways, your opportunities to work this muscle—the muscle to choose a helpful lens—will arise as you exercise your other mental fitness muscles, such as learning to self-assess your internal state (the subject of our next chapter).

It is obvious why the choice you make is so important. Whatever *your* core beliefs are, they are the building blocks of your all-powerful perceptual lenses. It's pretty simple: a helpful perceptual lens provides empowering energy. Such a lens increases your options and choices and expands your possibilities. Impeding beliefs and lenses are limiting. They decrease options and choices (often resulting in you being "stuck") and close down the possibilities of movement or action. Which will you choose? It matters. Your choices will change the trajectory of your leadership, career, and life.

HOW TO CHOOSE A HELPFUL PERCEPTUAL LENS

In my coaching practice, I ask every client to talk about the most important beliefs they hold about themselves, their family, work, money, and more. It's a way into understanding their perceptual lens. Often, this is the first time they've ever given this topic any thought, and many get stuck. It's not that they have no beliefs; they just can't "see" them. We work together to tease out these lenses. Some of the more common ones are listed here. Do any resonate with *you*?

Impeding Lens: "I'm not as competent as people think; I'm a fraud."
Usually this belief is not accurate. You hold it because you're highly critical of yourself. Deep down you simply think you are not good enough.

A better choice: "I can build confidence."

Instead of discounting your entire self as incompetent and fraudulent, turn it around and get more detailed and granular. Ask yourself, "Where, specifically, do I need to improve? Where do I need to shore up my knowledge or experience so I can be confident in my abilities?" That's a more helpful lens than walking around with an excuse for feeling like you're not good enough. In other words, we say, "You don't think you're confident. Okay, let's identify where—and then let's fix that."

Impeding Lens: "I am successful because I work harder and longer than anyone else."

This approach is not helpful for a couple of reasons. First, you are on the road to burnout, and while you are burning out you are going to miss out on your family, play time, rest, and life in general. Second, it could be a sign that you don't have the right aptitude for your job. Let's take a simplistic example to make the point. If somebody is an accountant and they don't have the aptitude, it's very hard for them to do the same amount of work as the guy in the office next door who loves the work and finds it comes easily to him.

A better choice: "How do I achieve balance?"

Instead of insisting that you work harder and longer than everyone else, switch your focus. Ask yourself: "How can I achieve similar results *and also* feel more in balance?" This will lead you to place more emphasis (thoughts, moods, and actions) on prioritizing, delegating more effectively, and leveraging the 80/20 rule, where 80 percent of your success stems from 20 percent of your efforts. That means you need to select lenses that allow that to happen.

So often we have a habit of overworking, or being a perfectionist, or spending much longer than needed without a measurably better result. Adding "balance" into your lens of productivity will lead you to a way of working that ultimately gets more done, more effectively, and sustains your well-being over the long haul.

(Potentially) Impeding Lens: "If I want it done right, I have to do it myself."

This lens is fine if you want to be an individual producer. Stay with it and you will be amazing. However, you will never leverage yourself and your skills to be able to develop people, or have two thousand people under you, because you won't be able to delegate. If you want to be a senior leader, this lens won't work. That said, not everyone wants to be a senior leader, and that's okay.

A better choice: Create a safe, secure, supported team.

If you do want to be a leader, you need to truly understand that you can't do it all by yourself. You need to accomplish your goals through others, and that means you need to create followership, and people won't follow you unless you make them feel safe, secure, and supported as you lay out the clear objectives you want them to accomplish. You start to do that by selecting the appropriate lenses we are going to talk about.

Whatever your beliefs, the majority were indoctrinated in you throughout your formative years. You learned and absorbed them from your parents, teachers, friends, and even the media—TV, movies, radio, newspapers—you consumed. Now, with adult eyes, you can reconsider and ask yourself: How are those beliefs serving you? What outcomes do they create? Do they consistently help you experience a better life for yourself and those around you? Do they build you up, and build others up, creating optimism, possibility, and a sense of opportunity?

Now that we have talked about some very common indoctrinated impeding perceptual lenses ("I am not good enough;" "other people can't be trusted"), let's take a look at three perceptual lenses that I have found to be essential to mental fitness.

HELPFUL LENS #1: A CHANGE MINDSET

Let's say you've decided you're out of shape, and it's time to lose some weight and tone up your muscles. You sign up at a local gym and meet your personal trainer. If you have a helpful perceptual lens, what would be your assumptions?

Well, you would believe:

- It is possible to improve your body (otherwise, you wouldn't be doing this).
- Working out at the gym will be an effective method (or else you would have chosen a different method). And,
- A trainer has information or guidance to share with you that will be new and useful (otherwise, you would do this on your own).

All of these helpful beliefs about the process and desired outcome work together to create openness, curiosity, and motivation as you arrive on your first day.

It's much the same when you embark on developing your mental fitness; it is important that your perceptual lens be useful rather than impeding. That includes making helpful assumptions about the process, about your ability to change and grow, and about the potential outcome.

Read the examples in the two columns in this chart. In each row, which belief or assumption underlies *your* own perceptual lens about developing your mental fitness? Put a checkmark next to your answers below. Only put one checkmark per row. If you are unsure, pick the one that feels true most often. If you really can't decide, then put your checkmark in column B.

A	B
___ People can change.	___ People rarely change.
___ I can change.	___ I can't change (or at least not much).
___ The mental fitness methodology can work for me.	___ The mental fitness methodology probably won't work for me.

If you checked all three in column A, great! Holding these three beliefs puts you in an open, curious mood that will accelerate your learning. I think of them as creating a "change mindset."

If you checked any of the items in column B, then your current perceptual lens is going to be working against you as you try to make changes. These indicate—at least to some degree—a more fixed or rigid viewpoint about yourself or about how things are.

Why is that a problem? Consider this scenario. Suppose that your perceptual lens is that your body "is what it is; it's not likely to change," and going to the gym is probably *not* going to help. But, you go to the gym anyway. Can you still get in shape by working out there? Well, you can certainly force your body to go through the physical motions of exercise. But, you'll be giving your body mixed messages:

Lift these weights now!   *This isn't gonna work.*
Run! Run faster!   *All this sweat and for what?*
Push harder!   *Damn, I don't have the right body for this.*

Any physical changes that *do* occur will take longer to achieve than if your beliefs were aligned with a change mindset. Further, the changes won't be sustainable over the long haul, because you won't have the motivation to continue. Overall, the lack of change mindset in this example is a kind of "decelerator" for you reaching your goal.

This might seem obvious. Why on earth would you go to the gym while believing you won't change? And yet, I see the equivalent every day as people try to change the more intangible parts of themselves. For example, have you ever said or thought the following?

"It's just how I am."

"I want to change, but nothing seems to work."

"I am someone who _____."

We tend to believe that however we are in the moment, however we have shown up in our lives so far, well, that's just who we are. We *hope* we can change. We want to change. But the key element is missing! We don't whole heartedly *believe*—without reservation or doubt—that we *can* change.

If your perceptual lens is one of doubt or skepticism, that lens will not *prevent* you from getting positive results, but it will take longer and feel much more difficult to achieve them. And if you believe you *cannot* change, then you absolutely won't. You'll succumb to the internal gravitational pull toward maintaining your own status quo. You'll be *stuck*.

Change Mindset and Growth Mindset

You may know the work of Stanford psychologist Carol Dweck. Dweck argues, correctly in my opinion, that people with a growth mindset believe their most basic abilities can be developed through dedication and hard work—brains and talent are just the starting point. This view creates for them a love of learning and a resilience. But it seems to me that you have to believe you can get better, i.e., you need to have a change mindset, the belief you can transform yourself for the better, before the growth mindset can kick in.

So, in that sense, what we are talking about here is a precursor to Dweck's concept. If you have a growth mindset, you're good. But if you don't, I suggest you consider working on developing it by changing your perceptional lens—especially as today's world gets more disruptive and chaotic.

Let's take a business example to hammer home the point. Consider this: Some 90 percent of the companies that were on the Fortune 500 in 1955 are no longer there, according to a study from the John M. Olin School of Business at Washington University, which estimates that 40 percent of today's Fortune 500 companies will no longer exist in ten years, victims of the inability to respond to market needs. To use the classic example, Blockbuster failed to adapt to streaming and is now just a memory. In contrast, Netflix, a primary reason that Blockbuster went out of business, is constantly evolving. In addition to streaming, it offers original television and movies through the service, is releasing original movies (such as *The Irishman*) into theaters, and is experimenting with adding audio streaming as well.

My view is that your "self" is not a fixed thing but rather something fluid and dynamic. It just seems fixed because you unconsciously work very hard to make it that way! You practice your same thoughts, moods, and behaviors day in and day out. No wonder you believe you are what you are. But your sense of self is the *result* of those patterns, not the cause. Your real self is much like a blank slate, or a scoop of clay that can be shaped any number of ways.

The change mindset holds that even though you have been a certain way in the past, it doesn't mean it has to be that way going forward.

Yes, you'll need to overcome habits and patterns. That's just the work to be done! And if you have a rigid mindset about changing yourself, you'll double down on your beliefs. ("I am who I am; it's just how it is.") However, if you have a change mindset, you'll relate to the challenges differently. You will see them as a normal part of being human.

Here are some ways to choose a change mindset as your helpful perceptual lens.

1. Never again entertain the thought "That's just who I am." Say instead, "That's the self I've practiced up until now. My real self can always change."
2. Try to catch yourself if you get discouraged and start thinking, "What if this doesn't work and I don't change?" In that moment, choose this frame instead: "What if it *does* work? What if I *do* change?" Then put your attention back on doing the actual *work* of changing.
3. If you get *really* discouraged and go to the place of "I'll never change," or "This will never work," then it's time to realize you've slipped to a victim mentality lens. With this sense of hopelessness, the core belief is "I can't" or "I'm not good enough." That simply will not serve you.

There are two parts to changing here. First is self-awareness. Understand what you are saying and doing to yourself. Then reframe your statements so they are positive. (I can; I will; I must.) And then take repetitive, corrective action to change.

HELPFUL LENS #2: POSITIVE EXPECTANCY

Let me give you a representative example of the positive expectancy lens. I am working with a brilliant PhD on changing her moods at work. Although she is ridiculously smart—she earned that doctorate in physics at a ridiculously young age—she is constantly fearful she won't measure up. That attitude makes her overly cautious and causes people to avoid working with her because she causes a bottleneck.

We were on the phone as she was reviewing some of the positive steps she had taken during the week to change her perceptual lens. She had done a great job, and yet she opened our call saying, "This is really hard to do."

I asked, "Do you believe in what we are trying to do here?"

"Yes."

"Do you believe you did a good job last week in changing?"

"Yes."

"Now, can you see by saying, 'This is really hard,' you are making it more difficult for you to change? You are picturing huge boulders in your way before you even begin."

I told her that going forward, we would work on changing her underlying belief to "It will be easy to have my authentic self come out at work."

Do You Expect Good Things to Occur?

Is *your* glass half empty or half full? When something is yet to happen, what do you typically *expect*? Do you say, for example:

- "This probably won't go well."
- "I doubt that this can really work out."
- "This is such a long shot."
- "They always… (or, they never…)"
- "Things never go the way I want."

I'm not talking about whether you engage in the process of planning ahead to assess and mitigate risk. I'm asking about your thoughts and beliefs around your *expectations*. Dwelling on what can and will go wrong, and how bad things are going to be when they do, are thoughts that are not serving you. In fact, they contribute to a self-fulfilling prophecy: as you expect, so you will mostly get.

For mental fitness, one of the *most* helpful perceptual lenses you can select is positive expectancy. You choose to believe in the probability of a desired outcome instead of a feared or undesirable one. You choose to believe, for example:

- In general, things work out, even when you can't see it in the moment.
- In most situations, it is most likely that a positive outcome will occur.
- In general, outcomes follow intentions, i.e., the more I choose to believe that a positive outcome will occur, the more likely that it will.

Now, a caveat. Positive expectancy is not the same as having an artificially Pollyannaish lens on life. Pollyanna thinking is a willful denial of reality, an unbalanced perspective in which everything is painted with a false positivity. There is a forced quality to it—paradoxically, a kind of rigidness or inflexibility in the way that this "positive" lens is applied.

Positive expectancy goes hand-in-hand with practical, pragmatic planning and action; it's not wishful thinking. Whenever you set out to do something, you think ahead; you anticipate and plan for potential risks and problems. But you don't do this in a state of anxiety or fear. You do not dwell on all the negative possibilities. Rather, you do your analysis—your due diligence—and you make necessary and responsible plans. And then you let it go.

From that point forward, as you execute your plan, and as things unfold, you actively manage your beliefs. You fully expect a good outcome. It's an experience of internal confidence. And it is indeed a choice. When you believe that a positive outcome will occur, your thoughts and moods will align to that outcome, as will your decisions and actions. All of that alignment increases the probability of the positive outcome that you have chosen to expect.

HELPFUL LENS #3: TRUST

Trust is absolutely essential to mental fitness; levels of trust align with levels of success. When you trust, you're open. When you're open, you connect with others. When you connect, people respond. And then, you get information and you are included in their processes. Building this kind of emotionally connective engagement develops rich followership, and that is essential to creating and sustaining forward movement in your organization.

However, trusting is difficult for many people. It touches their core in very primal ways. Beliefs that lead to trust, or distrust, are directly related to survival, and they begin to form at a very early age, even before we learn to speak. A baby comes into the world naturally trusting, because in order to survive, it must accept care provided by others. The beliefs and behaviors of the baby's caregivers—and circumstances of the baby's life—influence the baby. The very best outcome is when the baby feels safe and therefore learns trust.

But sometimes, care is inconsistent, or the baby (and later the child) suffers harm from a caregiver (intentionally or unintentionally), or the caregiver teaches the young person that the world is very unpredictable. Or, life events actually do bring harm. A perceptual lens is then formed, with the belief that to survive, extra protection is required. Distrust and suspicion are a way of protecting the self in a world that is seen or experienced as unsafe.

Attachment Theory: A Deeper Dive

A child's formation of trust in the early stages is usually referred to in the aggregate as "attachment theory," a set of concepts that explain the emergence of an emotional bond between an infant and a primary caregiver and the way in which this bond affects the child's development into adulthood. To reduce the concept to its essence, there are three distinct types of attachment: secure,

continued

anxious, and avoidant. The first is typically seen in those who had a healthy childhood. The second two can be formed as a result of trauma in early life, such as neglect, poor parenting, or other problems. You'll often find yourself, as an adult, responding in ways that mirror your childhood, and so it's helpful to be aware of that so you can make course-correcting moves.

There are two books I would recommend, if you would like to learn more: *Attached: The New Science of Adult Attachment and How It Can Help You Find and Keep Love* by Amir Levine and Rachel Heller and *Becoming Attached: First Relationships and How They Shape Our Capacity to Love* by Robert Karen.

It is important to understand that, at the time in life when these lenses *first* take shape, they serve a very real and vital purpose: they help ensure survival. The problem comes later when these lenses persist into adulthood, distorting our ability to accurately sense risk or threat. If the crippling perceptual lens of distrust is familiar to you, then you likely perceive risk or threat all or most of the time—even when it is not there. This lens limits your capacity to develop mutually beneficial relationships. It causes you to act with secrecy and suspicion—which then causes people to react to you in kind.

Of course, it is prudent to be wary when appropriate. You should always use your emotional intelligence to accurately assess your environment and circumstances. There are going to be times that distrust is called for. But it is not helpful to live with generalized distrust.

A lot of very good material has been written about trust in organizations. An excellent resource is Stephen M. R. Covey's work, *Speed of Trust*. He found that trust in an organization can be quantified and measured in three specific domains: the trust level inside the organization, the observable behaviors that create or destroy trust, and the economic impact of the trust level inside the organization. As Covey points out, less trust results in less speed and greater cost; more trust means you can move faster with less expense.

Your Trust Lenses Influence Others

For you to be an effective leader—to embody mental fitness—you must realize that your own personal perceptual lens around trust will create or destroy trust within your organization. If you want better economic outcomes for your team or company, then you should deeply examine and challenge your own lens around trust. So, what *is* your perceptual lens for trusting others? Here is a very straightforward way to consider your current lens—and choose an alternative, if your current one is lacking.

"Suspicious until."

With this lens, your default mode is to *dis*trust most everyone. You are suspicious of a person's (or organization's) motives, intents, or behaviors until such time as you get "proof" that you can trust them. When things go awry, your first thought is how that person or organization *intended* to cause you problems. This further reinforces your belief that you always have to watch your back.

Here's an example: You've just hired a new employee. If you are like most bosses, you will expect that a new employee has a certain level of competence and confidence (otherwise you would not have made the hire, right?). However, if you have a "suspicious until" mindset, then you do not *automatically* believe this. Even though you made the hire, you believe the employee is not competent (or not yet). You strongly believe you have to monitor and manage the new employee very, very closely, because they might make a mistake. At some point—it could be three months in, or a year—you may loosen up and feel that you can trust that the employee is going to deliver, because you have seen them do it perfectly for a while.

"Trust until."

With this lens, your default belief is that it is generally safe (and productive) to trust other people. You assume good intentions—or at least the absence of ill intentions. When things go wrong, your first thoughts are that there was a misunderstanding, or perhaps a lack of competence, but that the harm was an unintended outcome. You trust someone until there is a clear and well-grounded reason not to.

Let's use the same hiring example. You hire this person because of their competence and you say, "I trust she has the ability to deliver, and I am going to continue to think that unless (or until) she makes a big error or a big miss."

"Suspicious still."

When someone has broken your trust, are you done with them? Do you assume that they will break your trust again in the future? If you have a "suspicious still" perceptual lens, the answer is yes. Your perceptual lens is anchored to the specific incident or time when they broke your trust, and there is nothing they can ever do after that to regain it.

Here's how that would play out in our hiring example. The person you brought on board has proven themselves beyond reproach for years, after making a mistake which virtually no one else can remember. But you're still suspicious because you actually believe you can't trust others, that people will always fail you at some point; it's just a matter of time. And you, indeed, remember that long-ago mistake. You're firm in your thinking that you will never trust them, nor do you trust anyone. You just *know* that as soon as you stop looking over your shoulder, they are going to hurt you.

"Trust still."

This lens is often the least familiar of the trust lenses. With this lens, you make the conscious choice to trust someone *even after* they have given you reason not to trust them. You choose to regard the incident of broken trust as being in the past, and you do not assume it will be repeated in the future. This lens is not easy to achieve, because there is almost nothing in our culture or society that teaches this lens. Yet, research shows that it is one of the most powerful lenses you can choose to employ.

How does this work? Continuing our example: You hire someone who's qualified, and then they make a mistake. But when they do, you lend them even more trust. You say, "So you made a mistake today. It's okay." You then give them more instructions, or do whatever you have to do, so that they learn from the mistake. And then? You move on. You don't micromanage, or yank away the trust.

Let me stress that I am not speaking of blind trust here. You still need to use discernment. Discernment requires mindful attention on your part, because you have to read the actual specifics of a situation. With discernment, you consider multiple possible interpretations (i.e., look through multiple lenses) rather than automatically assuming you should not trust. You can always choose, situationally, not to trust someone or to proceed with a sense of prudent caution.

HELPFUL LENS #4: ACCEPTANCE OF "WHAT IS"

It was a Friday afternoon and I was in a local store trying on shoes when my mobile phone rang. It was Kelly, my operations director. She was extremely upset. I couldn't understand a word she was saying. I heard something about a house. I asked her to slow down and try again.

> **Kelly**: Your house is on fire!!
> **Me**: Okay . . . did you call the fire department?
> **Kelly**: Yes!!!!
> **Me**: Are the cats out of the house?
> **Kelly**: No! The firemen won't go inside to get the cats!
> **Me**: Okay, I'm coming there now.

My house was a good twenty minutes away. I finished paying for my new shoes. I felt calm. I *was* calm. There was nothing to be done. I thought, "This is 'what is.' My house is on fire." As it turned out, I couldn't even get to my street because there were several fire trucks and two ambulances, along with Red Cross representatives, policemen, and lots of camera crews. My house fire had been significant—to say the least.

I wanted to get to my cats, but the fire crews wouldn't let me near the house. A guy from the Red Cross came up to me. His nametag read "John," and he put his hand gently on my arm.

> **John**: I'm so sorry for your loss.
> **Me**: Thank you so much.

John [going into social work mode]: Loss is so difficult. I'm here to help you through this. Whatever you're feeling right now is completely normal . . .

Me: John, let me stop you. [I take his arm and use *my* social work voice.] John, I'm fine. Really. I'm fine.

John: No. You're in shock.

Me: John, if I were in shock I would be exhibiting the *symptoms* of shock. I would be pale. Weak, dizzy, or agitated. Breathing rapidly. Is your assessment that I am demonstrating these symptoms of shock?

John: No . . . you're not.

Me: Right. Because I'm not in shock. But my employee, Kelly, who was in the house when the fire started, is now traumatized. Kelly *is* in distress. Look at her. Can you please attend to her, and I will go talk to the fire chief?

As John went over to talk with Kelly, the fire chief told me that it was lucky that someone called the fire department when they did. Two minutes later, the roof would have collapsed on Kelly, and she would have been severely injured or killed. Within five minutes, the entire house would have been completely engulfed and destroyed. To this day, I remember how grateful I felt in that moment. My only concern in that moment was whether my two cats were okay. (It turned out they were fine.)

On that day, I maintained a perceptual lens of acceptance, or "what is." My gorgeous three-story home, built in the 1910s in the Queen Anne architectural style, had burned. The fire had been caused by careless roof workers who used a blowtorch to warm up the materials they were using on that cold day. There was tremendous—and expensive—damage. The building was not just my home; it also housed the office for my staff and client meeting rooms. As a result of the fire, my workplace and living space was under construction for months, inconveniencing me, my clients, and my staff. It would have been easy to slip into victim mentality. Blame bad luck. Blame it all on the roofers! Blame myself for having chosen this incompetent, neglectful roofing company in the first place.

But I didn't go there. I chose to maintain a perceptual lens of acceptance all the way through the reconstruction. No, I didn't want any of this. I didn't choose any of it. I certainly didn't like any of it. But it happened. In any moment that I felt even a whisper of blame or despair arise in myself, I quickly shut that down and chose the more helpful lens of acceptance. "This is just what is. I can't control that the fire happened. What *do* I have control over in this moment? Let me focus on that."

Focus on What You Can Control

If nothing else, you always have control of your perceptual lens—your perspective on the situation. You can control your thoughts, moods, and actions. Acceptance doesn't necessarily mean you feel *good* about what has happened. But you don't waste energy resisting, defending against, or ruminating about something over which you have no control. You let that part go. If you really get to true acceptance, you can feel peaceful even in the midst of all the turmoil.

Accepting "what is" frees up more of your energy to actually deal with the parts of the situation over which you *do* have control. In my case, I quickly came to see the entire situation through the lens of opportunities. The house had been needing repairs for some time. I had been wanting to remodel. And my home had been filled with visual reminders of a painful relationship that I had tolerated for too many years and had finally ended just two months prior. While I would not have chosen this timing to fix up my house, it had been given to me.

You accept what is.

That is not always easy, and it is not the only challenge you might face while working on this muscle.

POTENTIAL ROAD BUMP#1: YOU'RE ATTACHED TO YOUR STORY

When you get a new eyeglass prescription, you have to let the old glasses go. Sure, you can keep the frames—but there still has to be an actual replacement of the *lenses*. You can't just glue one lens on top of the other. I know that sounds ridiculous. But this is exactly what people often try to do when it comes to changing their *perceptual* lens.

You can't change your lens while wearing your current lens. The people who have the hardest time transforming their leadership, or their lives, are those who hold onto their own story very, very tightly. They are attached to it. Their self-image is dependent upon them being "the one who always _____." Fill in the blank any way you want. The one who's always right. The one who never gets what they want. The one who always achieves. The one who always cleans up after others. The one who's the smartest. The one who is always betrayed. When you are so locked into your own self-image, then a change of perceptual lens can feel destabilizing. If you aren't the one who always is this or that, or who does this or that, then *who are you?*

When you step into the unfamiliar territory of using a new lens, you need to be willing to "try" it out. *It's not going to feel normal to you.* On some level you will feel some relief—because you are choosing a lens that empowers you— but on another level you are likely to resist the feeling of change. I'm working with someone right now who is resisting. He is a senior leader in a large private company that has been family controlled for generations. The board of directors just brought in a new CEO, from outside the family, with a wildly different view on how to best move this company forward. In my opinion, the new CEO's vision is forward-thinking and spot-on. It will likely contribute to keeping the company in business for many more generations to come.

But the leader I was hired to work with hates the new ideas. And while he is used to running things from a command-and-control perspective, the new vision pushes authority way down the ranks, giving people much greater autonomy so that the company can move faster. This leader is having a great deal of trouble adjusting, because he does not want to change his style. He liked the way things were. The old way worked— for him—for the last fifteen or twenty years. He is openly defiant to the changes, and his colleagues find him whining, complaining, and presenting a victim mentality. It's draining for all of the people who work for him and for his peers, and he's blocking progress. He is not in alignment with the rest of the company.

My job is to help him transition to adopting a growth mindset. He will need to change, or leave. The new reality is, there is no longer any room for his kind of leadership in this company. Even though it was relevant just a year ago, it has now become outdated. Sometimes when I talk about situations like this, people ask if there is a middle ground between the old lens and the new. I don't think there's one answer to that; I think it depends on the company and the leadership. But if I'm leading that family-owned company, I'm not going to tolerate it. This leader is out of alignment with where the company has explicitly declared that it wants to go.

There are many ways to resist changing, and this executive showed many of them: intellectualizing, arguing, debating. Diverting, evading, avoiding. Complaining, excusing, rationalizing. The list just goes on and on. None of this is productive behavior.

If you've ever felt this way to any degree, the better approach is to recognize your discomfort for what it is: your ego's inner defenses against change. The solution? Acknowledge that discomfort while trying on the new lens—even though it feels odd, contradictory, or just plain impossible. You keep doing that again and again until the new lens can start to stay in place, and the new lens becomes the new you.

Initially, you aren't going to have "proof" that any of these helpful lenses will bring you better results than your current, impeding lens. You can only give them a try. Be curious, open, experimental. *Lean into it*. Doing so increases your options. And pay attention to what happens; observe your new results. Loosen up on your own story until you really get that *your story* is not *you*. That's the only way that true change can happen.

Key Points

- **You choose what you believe about yourself.** And it is indeed a choice.
- Perceptional lenses come in two flavors. **A helpful perceptual lens is empowering.** It increases your options and choices, and expands your possibilities. **Impeding beliefs and lenses decrease options** and often result in you being stuck.
- **Consistently challenge your perceptional lens** by asking two questions:

    1. Is this lens impeding or helpful?

continued

2. Did I choose this lens, or was imposed on me by the way I was brought up and/or past experiences?

- **There are multiple helpful lens** such as:
- **Having a change mindset.** You believe you can get better.
- **Positive expectancy.** You choose to believe in the probability of a desired outcome instead of a feared or undesirable one.
- **Trust.** You start with the expectation you can count on others.
- **Accepting what is.**
- Although it is difficult for many, **trust is absolutely essential to mental fitness.**
- **You can change.**

7

ACCURATELY
SELF-ASSESSING

Q: How do you know you are leading lightly?
A: Ask:

- How *you* feel (anabolic or not?)
- How *others* feel around you
- Someone you *trust*

Leading lightly is what arises from the consistent application of the mental fitness muscles. Self-assessing, one of those muscles, can lead you to see that you are not leading lightly because you are in a catabolic state. The more often you self-assess when you are triggered, the more quickly you can change and get out of that triggered state. Do that often enough, and leading lightly will be your new normal, your new natural state of being.

The muscle to self-assess your internal state is your skill in articulating your (1) moods, (2) physical sensations, and (3) thoughts—in the moment—while all three are occurring.

Mentally fit leaders do something truly remarkable: they can move through their day as if they are two different people simultaneously; as if they have two parts of themselves that are distinct—yet integrated—operating at the same time.

One part—the part that we can see—is in action, fully engaged with people and situations. The other is internal and private but no less powerful. This invisible part is like a detached observer, quietly and supportively watching and noticing all that is happening in the leader's internal landscape. This part is making adjustments in real time as necessary.

While the leader is outwardly engaged in conversations, work, meetings, etc., her unseen observer takes note of any inwardly shifting moods, physical sensations, and thoughts. It provides her with valuable self-assessment information; for example, "Am I shifting into a catabolic mood? Feeling tension? Frustration?" And, perhaps most powerfully, she can tune in to her own internal "running commentary"—her thoughts—with a detached clarity and objectivity. As an example, let's suppose she is sitting with one of her direct reports, Bill. Her inner commentary might go something like this: *"Why the heck can't Bill get to the point? He's been talking for twenty minutes—and I still have no idea why he is so upset!"*

What Is Your "Internal State"?

It's the running commentary of thoughts in your head; your moods and the emotions that you feel; and your physical sensations, such as muscle tension, rapid heartbeat, or a knot in your stomach.

But using the muscle to self-assess—tuning in and actually hearing her own inner commentary in real time—the leader then self-corrects: *"Oh. Wait. He's only been talking a few minutes. I must be really stressed about that board presentation I need to create. Okay. Deep breath. Concentrate on what he is telling you."*

What we are talking about here is the **skill of self-awareness**. When people first encounter this idea, they sometimes confuse it with certain negative psychological experiences. So, before we dive in more deeply, let's first spend a minute talking about what it isn't. Self-awareness is *not*:

- An out-of-body or dissociative experience
- That floaty/disconnected feeling where you "see yourself" as if from a distance
- The experience of being self-conscious or ill-at-ease, such as when you feel insecure, or that you don't belong
- A paralyzing state in which you overanalyze every little thought or fleeting emotion that runs through you

Self-awareness is not a negative experience; rather, it is a state of *keen, supportive awareness*. In this state, you notice, identify, and use your underlying operating system and perceptual lenses. This internal observing part is your helpful ally. As you develop the muscle to self-assess your internal state, you learn to continually gather three data points about yourself:

1. Mood
2. Physiology (Body Sensations)
3. Core Thoughts

When you self-assess your internal state, you become curious about what's there. You do your best to find or see what's going on, without any self-judgment or self-condemnation. Whatever you find, it's just *data*. But this is the most empowering and impactful data you will ever encounter. It will help you deal effectively and efficiently with every situation you face, as you saw with the leader who was getting cranky with her direct report because she was worried about something else (that had nothing to do with the person talking to her). And it's a tool that is there for the using; you just have to learn how.

HOW TO SELF-ASSESS

As you begin to develop this muscle, you'll find yourself in unfamiliar territory. It can seem strange at first, and you are bound to have a lot of questions such as: What am I looking for? How do I know I found it? And how useful is this, really? Over time, as you develop your skill, this ability to self-assess your internal state becomes automatic. It opens up a whole new lens for you. And in turn, that lens shapes how you move through life—in a very different, much more effective and joyful way.

We are going to look at each of the three data points of self-assessing: moods, physical sensations, and the core thoughts that are affecting your performance. You'll eventually find your own rhythm for assessing these three together, and ultimately you will do it so fast that it will be automatic.

Here's the process that I teach as you're getting started.

DATA POINT #1: YOUR MOOD

At any given moment, can you name what you are feeling—in an accurate and nuanced way? In my coaching practice, I have each client use my app, Mind-Mastery® for Mental Fitness™, to quickly check in with themselves and answer a (seemingly) simple question: "What is your mood right now?" The client does this check-in eight times every day, including weekends, for a whole week.

Later, when I look over all his entries, I usually see the same one or two answers over and over—especially on workdays! Typically, he will repeatedly use a word such as *anxious, nervous, overwhelmed, pissed,* or *stressed.* Or he may note that he feels simply "good" or "bad." Some clients write no answers at all. They are stuck. They truly don't know *what* they feel, or they are numb inside. Or, they simply cannot access this information about themselves when they first begin.

Like my clients, you probably have only a handful of general moods that you can readily recognize and describe. This is completely normal when you begin! You might feel "worried" or "anxious." Or maybe it's more "annoyed" or "ticked" or "frustrated." You could be someone who prides yourself on keeping a "positive outlook" on things, so you find that your mood is often "good" or "fine" or "GREAT!!!!"

Whatever your answers are, they are. There is no right or wrong, even if you have only one or two words to use. You just start where you are. Refrain from judging yourself, and then go on from there.

MindMastery® for Mental Fitness™

I wanted to make the process of achieving Mental Fitness as efficient as possible. That's why I wrote this book. And it is also why I created the MindMastery® for Mental Fitness™ app. It increases your self-awareness, the first step in building mental fitness, by reminding you to check in with your moods and thoughts at eight random points throughout the day. Random alerts to check in with your thoughts and moods are the foundation that lead you to recognizing catabolic energy as it unfolds in real time.

For our executive coaching clients and participants in our Mind-Mastery training, we offer a more advanced version of the app that incorporates deep brain-change methodology. Both our coaching and training go more deeply into the topics we've been discussing throughout this book. With repetitive engagement, the app will help rewire your brain as you direct it to change the way you think for the better.

You can download the free version of the app from the Apple App Store or Google Play.

Finding the Words

Every person's "mood vocabulary"—how they describe their inner experience of mood—is unique to them. And on top of that, every person feels different emotions, and at different intensity levels. For example, consider the basic emotion of fear. What is it like to feel a "low intensity" of fear? A moderate intensity? A high intensity? Here are some words that might be used to describe these differing levels. Your own mood vocabulary could be very different. This is just an example.

← **F E A R** →		
LOW INTENSITY	MODERATE INTENSITY	HIGH INTENSITY
Anxious	Dreading	Terrified
Worried	Scared	Panicked
Insecure	Alarmed	Petrified
Nervous	Distressed	Horror-struck

That chart was an example of the catabolic state of fear. What about an anabolic state? For example, you may think of the word "happy," or just plain "good." But again, there are so many nuances available. Consider the basic emotion of joy, at different levels of intensity. Again, these could be some examples of how you would describe what you are feeling:

← **J O Y** →		
LOW INTENSITY	MODERATE INTENSITY	HIGH INTENSITY
Pleased	Happy	Ecstatic
Satisfied	Delighted	Overjoyed
Content	Thrilled	Elated
Okay	High	Euphoric

I want you to get truly curious about your own mood vocabulary. It is part of really learning to pay attention to yourself in a new way. The more nuanced and specific you can be, the easier it then becomes to take the later step of identifying what needs to change.

The MindMastery® List of Feeling, Emotion, and Mood Words

Many of us do not differentiate our feelings very much. We use limited words to describe them, such as good, bad, happy, sad, anxious, or stressed. However, you probably know many more words for feelings than you actually use in daily life; you just don't think of them. As well, there are probably some new words you would use—if you only knew them! Use the MindMastery list of over 850 words to remind yourself of words you can use, while learning some new ones, too.

Go to www.jodymichael.com/feelings for our:

- Beginner List: getting started
- Main List: expanding your list
- Somatic List: words to describe your physiological sensations

What's Your Mood? An Exercise

As often as you can, check in with yourself, and continually ask the question "What is my mood right now?" In the beginning, you may find it very helpful to have a reference list of feelings or emotions, such as the Mind-Mastery® list (see box). Without using a list, you may not be able to readily name what you feel, but you might *recognize* it when you see it in a list. Let's try the exercise now. Pick up a pencil or pen and ask yourself: "What is my mood right now?" Write down your answer below.

If you find yourself resistant to this practice, please remember the context. This is not an abstract exercise. Nor will it make you soft or "touchy-feely." Again, we are gathering data. Just information! You are developing your muscle of self-observation and self-assessment.

What's the point? You are gathering data about yourself that, later, you will be able to use to rapidly shift out of a triggered mood that's hindering your performance. Remember the example about the leader's frustration with her direct report Bill who she thought had been talking for twenty minutes without getting to a point? The moment she understood what was behind her impatience—anxiety about her board meeting—she was able to shift past it and concentrate on what her lieutenant was saying, instead of snapping at him.

For now, you're just building your skills one step at a time. If you were working out in the gym, this would be like isolating your triceps, or quads, or any specific muscle that needs development.

DATA POINT #2: YOUR PHYSIOLOGICAL STATE

Your body can be tremendously useful in assessing your internal state. After all, the idea of catabolic and anabolic energy is based on actual physiological processes occurring in your body. Think about when you are angry. What happens? Your heart races; your breath comes faster; your face may flush with increased blood flow, and your muscles tense up. Your body is getting ready to move: fight or flight!

When you are nervous or anxious, you could experience these same signs; or, you might find yourself holding tension and stress. The point is, catabolic energy creates physical discomfort. We call this "somatic distress." It can be acute, as when you are severely triggered. Or, it can be more of a chronic experience, such as daily headaches, backaches, digestive problems, fatigue, and the like.

The reason you want to check on your internal state at random intervals is that you want to understand what is going on with you in the moment. This builds both self-awareness and emotional intelligence, powerful skills to develop in leadership.

When our somatic distress becomes chronic, we often adapt by becoming numb to it. When we do, we only occasionally feel any uncomfortable or painful sensations. Or, we know that they are there, but we find a way to ignore them and push through. But if we are to become mentally fit, we have to start listening to the body and accept that *at all times* it provides us with meaningful data.

Some people are more naturally attuned than others to the physical sensations that they feel. When I ask, "What do you notice in your body?" these people can readily identify and describe a pain, ache, or tight spot; or they can note that their breathing, heart rate, or blood pressure have changed.

However, more often I see that people are disconnected from their bodies. Is that true for you? You may be aware of a few aches and pains. But, as with your moods, if you are always identifying the same sensation over and over, and you are not doing anything about it, you are forfeiting a potential advantage. You have an opportunity to develop your awareness and improve your performance.

> ### What You Need to Know About: Physical Pain
>
> Every time you feel your back getting tight, or a pit forming in your stomach, you need to stop and identify the source of the pain. That pain is trying to tell you something.

You learn to self-assess physical sensations in much the same way as you did when you were self-assessing your mood: you have to check in with yourself. Your key question is now: "What sensations do I feel or notice anywhere in my body right now?" You might want to reference the "Somatic List" section of the MindMastery® List of Feelings, Emotions, and Moods on the JMA website (www.jodymichael.com/feelings).

You'll need to do this at random, multiple times throughout each day—noticing fluctuations and changes. If you find this difficult, or you tend to notice the same thing over and over, then I recommend a very effective practice called a "body scan" (see sidebar for instructions). This is about paying attention in a new way, and the body scan exercise methodically directs your attention throughout your body, step by step.

How to Do a Body Scan

Emotions live in the body and show up in the body. For example, if someone feels shame, it is generally expressed in the person's face. Their face may get red, or hot. When you get angry, your muscles tighten and your chest gets bigger. Some emotions can be observed from the outside, but on the inside, our internal experiences of these expressions can cover quite a range. The body scan is a systematic way to check for physical sensations, typically working from your toes up to your head. There is no judgment. There is no intent of effort to change anything. You simply observe as objectively as you can.

Step 1: Prepare

Take a moment to settle yourself:

- Sit comfortably with your posture straight, but not rigid. Or, lie down.

- Keep your legs and feet uncrossed.

- Close your eyes.

- Bring your attention to your body's contact with the chair and floor, such as the bottoms of your feet, your butt, your back, your hands.

- Take a few gentle breaths (deep, if you can, but don't force it).

Step 2: Scan your body

Slowly bring your attention to each part of your body listed below. For each one, notice any sensations such as tension, pain, coldness, warmth, numbness, tingling, etc. (or perhaps notice that there is no sensation at all). Two reminders: Don't judge what you find and don't rush; this is a practice in paying attention and detecting physical sensations.

What you scan:

- Feet, ankles
- Lower legs, knees, upper legs, thighs
- Lower abdomen, upper abdomen
- Chest
- Shoulders
- Throat
- Upper arms, lower arms

- Hands
- Back of head, skull, ears
- Neck
- Chin, jaw
- Cheeks, nose
- Eyes
- Forehead

Step 3. Close and return

Before finishing, run your attention across your entire body for a final quick scan.

- Bring your attention back to your breath for three to four breaths.

Open your eyes, and gently stretch.[1]

DATA POINT #3: YOUR THOUGHTS

Now we come to the most challenging, but rewarding, part of the self-assessment muscle: learning to identify your thoughts. The payoff is absolutely worth the effort that you'll put in. In fact, if I had to single out one component of mental fitness as being *the* most important and impactful, it's this one.

---

1 The body scan exercise has been around for a long time and is used by many teachers, coaches, and programs. There are many recordings available to guide you. You can search YouTube for "body scan meditation," use a meditation app, or try any of the following resources:
- 3-minute body scan: https://www.mindful.org/a-3-minute-body-scan-meditation-to-cultivate -mindfulness/ or download the free app "UCLA Mindful"
- 20-minute body scan: Download the free app "Mindful Moments by Cleveland Clinic"
- 45-minute body scan: UC Sand Diego Center for Mindfulness website: https://health.ucsd .edu/av/mindfulness/45MinBodyScan07mono.mp3

Why is it the most important? Because our thoughts are what create our response and are the reason for our reactions. It's not the event that actually causes our response; it's our thoughts about the event. So, you need to understand your predilections for thinking in habitual ways. Otherwise, nothing will change.

When you can begin to identify your thoughts, you can start to see your underlying patterns, and identify the core perspectives, beliefs, or attitudes that you have. That's why making the effort to develop this muscle is so important. Maybe the easiest way to think about it is to draw an analogy to a dandelion. You're not going to be effective in creating a beautiful backyard if you go out with your scissors and just cut off dandelion heads over and over again. The dandelions are going to keep popping back up. You have to dig them out at their roots. Your unproductive thoughts are the root system and, just like in your backyard, you need to get rid of them completely.

Words and Thoughts

When it comes to communications and thoughts, one of the exercises I do in my workshop is to hand everyone a piece of paper and a pen and say, "I going to give you a word, and I want you to write down the first five words that come to mind. Don't edit. Just write it down as quickly as you can. The objective here is speed." (Between you and me, the other objective is I don't want them overthinking.)

Then I give them a word like "education."

When we go around the room to see what each person has written, we find a whole gamut of answers. We hear everything from "apple, teacher, important" to the very opposite, such as "waste of time, debt, overrated."

The purpose of the exercise is to make this point: We're using just one word, and some people are triggered by it, and some are filled with love—all with the same word. That's why we need to always understand not only our internal monologue, but read the reactions and body language of others.

Almost all of the time, you have a dialogue going on inside your head. You think of this voice as you or your *self* and you have thoughts such as:

- That was *annoying!*
- How will I ever get this done in time?
- Why does she keep doing that to me?
- That sucked!
- Does he think I'm stupid?
- Maybe I really am stupid.

Remember back in chapter 4 we talked about our special "camera" that could (hypothetically) capture the thought bubbles of your internal thinking? It showed running commentary about the experiences you are having, and how you are interpreting them. For example, recall my client Joe's internal diatribe, also back in chapter 4 when his boss was dictating the unwanted last-minute assignment for Joe to put together a report. Here's what that camera revealed:

> *"I can't believe this. What the hell? Is he out of his mind? Does he think I have no life? Does he think he can just order me around? No respect. I am sick and tired of people never respecting me.*
>
> *"Story of my life. I should say something to him. No, no, control yourself. Don't blow. You can't afford to blow right now! Keep it together, Joe! Oh my god, what did he just say. I missed that. Shit! And I can't ask him to repeat it. He already thinks I'm an idiot. He's just looking for any reason to get rid of me.*
>
> *"Good, he's finally gone. I gotta go tell Susan about this. She is not gonna believe it. This guy is a joke."*

Now if we had asked Joe to identify his own thoughts for us, he probably would have said a few things like this:

- Well, I had a conflict with my boss.
- He told me to do something. It wasn't fair.
- I was so mad about it!

Look at those three sentences carefully. I call them *reporting*. When my clients first try to identify their thoughts, this is usually the type of thing they say. They tell me what was going on, what the situation was, and what they thought about the situation. Unfortunately, it is not the information we are looking for. *Reporting* is merely describing what we are doing, or what others in the situation are doing. That's what journalists do, they tell the story of what happened.

As a coach, when I am working with the client to build their mental fitness, I could not be less interested in the story! I do not care about what happened, at least not as it relates to identifying thoughts. Reporting is not going to help you develop mental fitness. In fact, it works against you!

Reporting does not get to what is actually going on in your mind, the things that were occurring while the event was happening. You need to get past the reporting and go deeper, to your actual internal core thoughts. These are generated by your underlying operating system and perceptual lens. This is why my MindMastery® for Mental Fitness™ app randomly asks you to stop *in the moment* to try to identify your thoughts. When you think about an event later, you are more likely to get into reporting.

To develop this skill without the app, you will need to stop many times in the day, check in with yourself, and ask: "What are my thoughts right now—in this very moment?" Learning to do this is somewhat like tuning into a radio channel if you have an old—i.e., nondigital—device. You have to keep fiddling with it until you get clarity. But once you've learned it, you can tune in easily, instantaneously, any time you need. And, that's great! You want to grow your awareness, and observe any patterns that show up over and over again, so you can identify triggers that cause you to react suboptimally.

How to Tune in to Your Thoughts

This stream-of-conscious exercise is one good way to tune in to find out what is going on with you, and it could not be simpler. All you need is a piece of paper and a pen. You just start writing down everything you are thinking at that very moment, even if it's nonsense, such as "I hate writing this." As you go, you're not editing anything; you're just writing free-flow.

Do not let your pen leave the paper at all! And don't stop until you have filled the entire page.

You will find that there is a whole lot of useless—and repetitive—garbage in your everyday thinking. (We could be using so much more of our brains than we do! But that's another subject altogether.) But, you will also find

1. clues to what is actually going with you, and
2. potential patterns that are impeding your progress.

For those who were able to do this automatic writing exercise effortlessly, great! Here's what I want you to do. Save the paper. Don't throw it out. Repeat this exercise two to three times. Do it at different times of the day over a period of a week or two. When you are finished, go back and read all your thoughts over multiple days. Then, I'd like you to analyze the data dispassionately. No judgment. Simply look to find repeated thought patterns.

There should be repeated threads that emerge. When you're finished doing that, you'll move to the next level. You'll now start to hunt for your core lenses. Those deep-seated beliefs, indoctrinated perspectives, that may or may not serve you. That lens will be a catalyst to habitually shape the thoughts you have with yourself. For example, a common core belief people have about themselves is "I am inadequate." That underlying belief can spring repetitive thoughts having you question your competence, your worth, or yourself in comparison to others. A common core belief people have about others is "People cannot be trusted." Thoughts that arise from this lens would question and assign negative intent to the actions of others.

Look carefully for what lenses are shaping your perspectives, behaviors, and quality of life. These lens are very valuable data to mine, they will help you get a glimpse into your underlying operating system. They will help you identify your helpful versus impeding belief systems.

Now, some of you may have trouble hearing your thoughts. You may get frustrated, listening—and hearing nothing. Be patient. You've been suppressing your thoughts or pushing them away, probably for a while, so you need to keep working at this. You need to give yourself permission to have your thoughts. If I am describing what you are experiencing, please repeat this exercise daily until your thoughts become audible. Over a period of time, you should begin to hear them.

The thoughts are there. In fact, experts estimate we have on average sixty to eighty thousand thoughts every day—most of them repetitive. That's an average of twenty-five to thirty-three hundred thoughts per hour! Other experts estimate a smaller number of fifty thousand thoughts per day, which translates to about twenty-one hundred thoughts per hour. It's doubtful that during the time you set aside to do this assignment you experienced no thoughts. They were there. You just couldn't hear them—yet.

Now, if you continue to have difficulty with hearing your thoughts, you might be operating in a state of dissociation. That's a clinical term, meaning you're checked out and you really don't feel. It happens to some people. If you are one of them, I very strongly recommend that you work with an experienced licensed psychotherapist who specializes in this targeted area.

The point here is that it's absolutely essential that you learn to hear and articulate your internal monologue so that you can begin to create some internal separation from the parts that are not helping you. Once you've made the start by identifying *any* of your thoughts, you can then refine your skill by further examining what is going on with you in any given moment. What I really want you looking for—trying to identify—are the core thoughts that are generating your current mood and physiology. Those core thoughts could be catabolic or anabolic, and of course it is the catabolic ones that we ultimately will want to challenge and change.

As it turns out, people's core thoughts are remarkably similar. You could say they are variations on universal themes. There are a whole lot of judgments. Assumptions. And, impeding beliefs. Here's a sampling of what I typically see in executives:

Catabolic
- "I'm right, they're wrong."
- "I must be the best."

- "They're out to get me."
- "What if I fail?"

Anabolic

- "I can do this."
- "What an opportunity!"
- "What am I not seeing?"
- "I trust you."

The key to learning to identify your core thoughts—just like with identifying your moods and your physical sensations—is to practice frequently throughout each day, many times per day, every day. Use my app, or use your own method, but in any case, be sure to jot down whatever you identify. Later, look over what you've written. For one thing, make sure you are truly capturing thoughts and not simply reporting. Second, start looking for the themes or patterns. They are there. Your catabolic moods are driven by a few core thoughts (beliefs). Pretty soon, when you find yourself in a catabolic energy state, you will know what to look for—your own "usual suspects."

Here's how this process could work. Start by asking:

Step 1A: **Are you in a bad mood or good mood?** Catabolic or anabolic? We start with mood because it's the easiest, most elemental part to identify.

Step 1B: **What is your actual mood?** Name it (i.e., anxious, dreading; happy, ecstatic). Refer to the list at www.jodymichael.com/feelings.

Step 2: **What physical sensations are you experiencing in your body?** Locate them, name them.

Step 3: **What are your thoughts in this moment?** Write them down.

Step 4: **Which thoughts *created* your present state** (mood, plus physical sensations)? Don't report on what's happening; try to get to the core patterned thoughts driven by your perceptual lens.

WHEN YOU NEED HELP

As you begin to develop your muscle to self-assess your internal state, you are likely to encounter a few predictable road bumps. This is especially true if you have never spent much attention on emotional intelligence, self-awareness, mindfulness, introspection, or the muscles of mental fitness. These road bumps are best worked through with individual coaching from someone who can be an objective thought partner with you. There is just no getting around the fact that when you are a novice and you make these mistakes, it will be very hard to see that for yourself. It's just the nature of the beast. You will think you are applying the skills correctly, but you probably won't be. After a while, you will wonder why you are not getting results, why nothing is changing.

When you need assistance in developing this muscle—or any of them, really—it is critically important that you choose someone whose perceptual lens is different from yours. They will look at things from another perspective and will be able to explain that other view to you. They also will be able to see your lens for what it is, and then help you see it too. They won't jump into your story with you, or get enmeshed in your mood by commiserating or engaging in an unproductive session of complaining; nor will they falsely cheer you on so that you keep making the same self-sabotaging mistakes.

It's not that they will be coldly detached; in fact, a good coach is going to have high emotional intelligence and be very adept at building trust with you. But think about it: if your coach has the same blind spots as you, or gets emotional about the same things you do, or holds the same viewpoints as you, then you're going to get commiseration, not coaching! Said differently, you don't want a yes-man as your coach; you want someone who will supportively challenge you and hold up a mirror. One more thing to keep in mind in choosing this person: they must be someone you can be vulnerable with, someone you can deeply trust.

POTENTIAL ROAD BUMP #1: YOU CAN'T IDENTIFY YOUR MOOD

So, you have started to check in with yourself to identify your mood, and . . . there is nothing there. Nothing good, nothing bad. You just can't find any mood to identify. It all feels pretty much neutral. Should that happen, you begin to feel frustrated with the practice itself. Or bored. Or annoyed! Your motivation wanes, and you start pulling back from working this muscle.

When you can't find any mood at all, it's going to be for one of two very different reasons. One relates to an anabolic state; the other to a catabolic state:

Anabolic: You are fully engaged, absorbed in the flow of whatever you are doing.

Catabolic: You are numbed out; you are cut off from feelings and moods.

When you are deeply absorbed in some activity that has your full attention, with no catabolic emotional aspect, then you won't likely be able to identify any one specific emotion. Here's an example. You are listening to a podcast on a topic that you find fascinating. There's no trigger, no mood state; you're just absorbing information. We can call this state simply "full engagement," or "engaged." You are lost in concentration, focus, or flow. Other examples of full engagement are the times that your body is at play. You're dancing, doing hobbies, playing sports, having sex—you're just in the flow of the activity. Or maybe for you, you find flow working in spreadsheets or crunching numbers.

But please note the difference: if, say, you were doing your taxes, you might be absorbed *and* in a catabolic mood state of frustration or confusion. So, please be discerning. The *anabolic* state of engagement is an experience of losing track of time because you were so involved and connected to your activity.

Now, about that other "moodless" state: being numbed out. This is going to be hard, because if you are numbed out, it is going to be very difficult for me to convince you that you are. People who are numbed out are in denial, and denial is one of the most difficult barriers to break through. You tell yourself—and everyone else—you are fine.

Know this: If you have no moods, emotions, feelings, and you are not in a state of flow, then *you are in a catabolic state of being numb.* Your pain and distress are so intolerable to you that you have dissociated from it. You feel nothing, so you can protect yourself from feeling bad. How can you know? The fact that you rarely feel anything is a primary sign. Here is something else that happens: you don't have an emotional reaction to events and circumstances that, for almost anyone else, would likely provoke some kind of feeling (even if it is a short-lived emotion, because they have applied their mental fitness muscles). For example, suppose you just received an extremely negative performance review; your boss told you in very clear terms that you are failing at a core part of your job. Instead of you feeling any surprise, anger, disappointment, or sadness, you feel nothing, or very little.

If you suspect that you are numbed out, then I strongly encourage you to seek the support of a qualified, licensed psychotherapist. Numbing out is shutting down. It is living without being truly alive. Please understand that you are in the ultimate form of catabolic "flight"—even if you have no idea what you are fleeing from. You will need professional support to break out of this state.

POTENTIAL ROAD BUMP #2: YOUR IDENTIFIED MOODS ARE "FALSE POSITIVES"

I have met many people who say that they are "very positive, incredibly positive" people. They're proud of their positive thinking. They just push negative thoughts and moods away. In fact, they are one of the most positive people they know!

That's good, right? That's mental fitness? Isn't that what this book is about? Unfortunately, no. It's not. If you believe that you are always extremely positive, always looking on the bright side, always able to turn lemons into lemonade—then I am talking to you here. Please listen carefully! There *is* such a thing as a "false anabolic" mood state. It is very tricky, very slippery, to identify. Your mood seems to be anabolic—good, positive, upbeat—but in fact, it is not, because it is based on underlying catabolic thinking. It is actually based on pervasive, hard-to-access fears.

This is so hard for you to see in yourself. So, let's look at some extremes, where it is easiest to observe. One type of extreme false anabolic state is

Pollyanna thinking. It's the "Stepford Wives" phenomenon. It is the complete denial that there is anything out of order in the present *perfect picture* of happiness. It's the fake happy face that covers up the deep family dysfunction, frightening financial struggles, the pain of adultery. Listen: denial is never, ever an anabolic response! Denial is a refusal to look at, take in, or deal with something difficult. This avoidance comes from an unrecognized place of fear. It is a form of shutting down, and it creates a false insulation with the notion that this will provide protection from all the unpleasantness in the world.

A second type of extreme false anabolic state is the person who is well-tempered to a fault. Whatever happens to, and around, this person, she always responds, "I'm just going with the flow. *It's all good.*" This attitude is often found in people who avoid conflict and who are usually overly accommodating of others' needs and wants. In addition, this attitude can sometimes be seen in people who believe themselves to be highly spiritually evolved. They rationalize that everything is out of their hands anyway, and they're just along for the ride, so why get upset?

Whatever the basis of a person's avoidance, they seek to prevent any internal disruption to their own personal sense of inner peace. In reality, this strategy is another form of rose-colored glasses (denial). Even more damaging, it reflects a profound lack of personal accountability.

False anabolic mood states are always about avoidance. The big problem is that avoiders rarely know that they are avoiding. Furthermore, if you give them feedback about their patterns of avoiding, they try to avoid hearing that feedback! So, it can be very difficult to break through to them.

Here's what I know: the only way to develop and genuinely maintain predominantly anabolic thoughts and moods is through personal development work. There are any number of ways to do this—my mental fitness method is just one; regular meditation practices are another—but in all cases, you must observe and change your underlying operating system and perceptual lens, ultimately changing your brain. No one ever became mentally fit through a strategy of avoidance!

POTENTIAL ROAD BUMP #3: YOU DON'T
FEEL ANYTHING IN YOUR BODY

Just as with moods, you may be challenged, initially, to sense what is going on in your body. You try to identify things going on with your body such as pain, tension, changes in breathing or heartbeat, and so on, but you don't really find anything. It all seems pretty much just fine. Or, you can sense that nagging little ache in your back or knee, but that's always there, so it doesn't seem like very helpful information.

If you don't notice any variations from one check-in to the next then this skill is something you'll really need to pay attention to. It may simply be that you are just not accustomed to doing it (like when you first learn to "tune in" to your thoughts; it's a very similar process). Or, you may be someone who tends to use avoidance as a defensive tactic in work and life. (If your body really is that Zen inside, then I'm betting that you have a solid and regular mindfulness practice that you have been doing for years.) I'm sorry to sound like a broken record, but if you feel nothing in your body, that is not necessarily a good thing. It likely signals being numbed out, shut down.

In a truly anabolic state, your body will feel specifically good—there is a relaxed but palpable sense of engagement and presence. But when you feel *nothing* in your body? That lack of sensation is your data point! It's telling you that you are numb. You have disconnected from the body's signals. Being numbed out is a common form of disconnection and it is a catabolic energy state. There is something wrong.

What should you do about it? For one thing, you can engage in activities that help you directly connect with your body, to literally generate physical sensation. Examples include getting a massage or other therapies that work directly with your physical body. But don't just be a passive, checked-out recipient, and don't distract from the experience by chatting with the provider during therapy. Pay conscious attention to the felt experience of receiving that therapy. Notice what your skin and muscles feel like throughout.

You can also engage in physical exercise or activities. The key, again, is to use each experience as a genuine opportunity to notice what your body is experiencing. Practices such as yoga, Pilates, or walking often work well. Strenuous exercise is less ideal because your attention is likely to be diverted to making effort rather than really noticing the nuances of the body's sensations.

If you really feel blocked, then I recommend that you seek the support of a qualified licensed psychotherapist. Often, a persistent disconnection from the body is the result of physical and/or emotional trauma that has occurred earlier in life. The mind creates a strong barrier for a protective reason.

HOW LONG WILL IT TAKE ME TO CHANGE?

It's common to wonder how long it will take you to change. The short answer is that some people can experience profound change in a matter of weeks; others may take six months or more. However, this is a superficial response, and not the best way for you to think about your efforts to change. Let's reframe the question in a way that's much more useful.

"Change" isn't just one thing. Different elements of change—resulting from your development of your mental fitness muscles—will show up in different ways and according to their own timelines. For example, there are going to be a set of constructive changes that your stakeholders experience as they interact with you. There will also be intangible (or internal), beneficial changes that you experience within yourself—psychologically, emotionally, and physiologically.

Of course, you can see tangible, positive changes, such as getting a promotion or other form of recognition. But there is a deeper level. Truly sustainable change occurs within you at the subconscious level, as a deep integration of new ways of thinking and moving in the world. You've perhaps heard of this progression of how people learn: we move through stages of "unconscious incompetence" to "conscious incompetence," then to "conscious competence," and finally, in mastery, "unconscious competence." That is the progression you want to go through here.

If you want to create change quickly, then consider that some of the factors involved in the speed of change are within your control, and some are not. For example, if you've had prior exposure to some of the ideas you're learning here, then you may catch on more quickly than other people. Obviously, prior exposure is not in your control; it's just "what is." So, I recommend that you put your attention and energy on what are in your control: repetition, attention, a passion for change, consistent focus, and (when appropriate) choosing to engage qualified support.

Key Points

- **Your internal state is the running commentary in your head**; your moods and the emotions that you feel, as well as your physical sensations, such as rapid heartbeat and shallow breathing.
- **Self-assessing your internal state means that at any given moment you can "observe" yourself** and articulate what you find.
- To discover your internal state, you **ask: What am I thinking right now; what is my mood; what do I feel in my body?**
- **Learning to identify your thoughts is the most important** and impactful part of mental fitness.

8

ENGAGING WITH MULTIPLE PERSPECTIVES

Q: Is it as "simple" as making sure one of the lenses you are trying on is leading lightly?

A: No.

But you do have to believe the leading lightly is possible—and desirable. Because it is the state that arises from the consistent application of the muscles, and the change of brain patterns, you will need to work on the limiting lenses that are active within you. In my experience, both personally and as a coach, most people have one to three core lenses that get in their way, not ten or twenty. Now, one of the things that could get in the way is your belief that leading lightly doesn't feel right because you have been brought up believing that leading is difficult, and should feel that way.

But many things "don't feel right" when they are new. If we aren't willing to tolerate discomfort (mental, emotional, physical) during the process of changing brain patterns, then change will not happen.

The muscle to engage with multiple perceptual lenses is your skill in discovering—and employing— divergent perspectives.

Let me tell you a story about me and one of my trusted team members at Jody Michael Associates, Naomi. It happened a few years back. As you read, ask yourself: Who do you believe was right, and who was wrong?

I was scheduled to lead a high-profile workshop for over fifty senior executives at a Fortune 200 tech company. After months of preparation, I was ready for my company, JMA, to shine. But about a week before the workshop, Naomi brought me some unwanted news.

"We have a problem," she said. The workshop was to include, as always, our proprietary MindMastery® for Mental Fitness™ app. The first version of the mobile app had been created several years before apps were as popular and prevalent as they are today. It had been developed rapidly on a shoe-string budget and it lacked bells and whistles. But it worked! And it worked well. It had served as a centerpiece of our workshop and coaching program.

For months, Naomi had been overseeing a major upgrade to the app—our version 2.0. Technology innovation is a key part of my company's brand—and technology innovation is also central to my coaching offering—so I was proud and excited about revealing this newer revision. Version 2.0 was sophisticated, even sexy! It had much more functionality, a robust new back-end platform to support more users, and a classy new JMA-branded design. I was excited! We were aiming to launch version 2.0 in time to use it at my workshop at the tech company. These participants would have a naturally critical eye about any technology I might present. The app had to be good.

Naomi was managing the project—the software development contractors, the testing, and the like—to get us to the finish line. Then came the unwanted news. She told me: "We are working on some bugs we found during testing. There is a strong chance version 2.0 will not be ready in time for the workshop. Be prepared that we may have to use the older version."

I was not happy to hear this. And Naomi's daily reports throughout the week were hardly more encouraging. Still, I held out hope. *It had to be version 2.0.*

The day before the big workshop, Naomi strongly advised me against unveiling the updated version. The bugs we had found had been resolved just that morning. And although the app was functioning, the risk of additional unforeseen problems was too high—she couldn't guarantee a smooth launch—and, to state the obvious, it would not be good to have our technology fail in front of a technology company.

Do not go live, she said. *Use the existing version.* Which was exactly the version I did not want to use.

What was I going to do? I paused to consider. Naomi had always been an outstanding performer. But I had observed her many times—in making both work and life decisions—to be risk averse. I knew myself to be quite comfortable with risk. I wondered how risky the launch *really* was. After all, the app had been stabilized; it was working.

In my assessment, the win of presenting our state-of-the-art app at the workshop would be big, while any loss would be minor. My client—as a tech company—would forgive a small bug here and there. In the world of software technology, it is standard practice to launch a product to millions of users with small known issues that would be fixed later. Businesses can't succeed if they delay introducing a new product until everything is perfect. The world is too competitive. Further, I was certain that the older version of the app would seem too simplistic to my workshop participants. Conversely, the new version's elegance and sophistication were completely aligned with my company's brand.

I came to a decision. All things considered, launching the new version was worth the risk. I told Naomi to go live with version 2.0.

The next day, with the workshop well underway, our big moment arrived. It was time to introduce the app to the participants. I told them how to download it and I waited as fifty people all pulled out their company phones.

It took all of thirty seconds for someone to say that they couldn't get the app to load. Then a second person said it, and then a third. Within five minutes, it was clear that half the people in the workshop—every one of them tech-savvy—could not access the app.

We later learned the company's firewall had blocked access to the app. We ended up reverting to the older version to take care of the needs of the workshop participants and our other clients.

RIGHT OR WRONG?

In retrospect, who do *you* think was right? Naomi or me?

It's a trick question. And not a very useful one. In a very real way, we were both right. Version 2.0 actually *was* ready to use (my perspective). And, we really did need additional testing for a smooth launch (Naomi's perspective). Upon reflection, these perspectives did not have to be mutually exclusive.

A week after the workshop, Naomi and I sat down to see what we could learn from what happened. We concluded that *each* of us had been locked into our own particular perspectives. We had both regarded the situation as binary. It was either/or: EITHER go live with version 2.0 (me), OR do not go live (Naomi). Neither of us had thought about the situation with curiosity, or with a flexible lens. It was yes or no. Go or no-go. My way or Naomi's way.

> *The lens you use impacts what you see, what you don't see, and how you respond.*

Naomi and I both missed the opportunity to use a key mental fitness muscle: to discover multiple perspectives, perspectives beyond the ones we initially held. In retrospect, we came to understand that we had not (individually or together) done any of the following:

- Approach our apparent predicament with a mood of *curiosity*
- Loosen up on what we "knew" to be the right decision
- Seek to discover multiple viewpoints beyond our own

Had we exercised greater mental fitness, we might have had a completely different outcome! We might have discovered a third perspective or lens. As just one example, we could have thought to *involve the client* as a participant in the launch testing.

With that perspective, we could have easily reached out to a number of people inside the organization. As it happened, I already had strong, well-established business relationships there. My contacts would have been happy to do a quick test of the new app before the workshop. The firewall problem would have been found and addressed, leading to smooth sailing in the workshop.

The way Naomi and I reacted is typical of how many business executives handle this kind of situation. Naomi was locked into her perceptual lens about *herself*. And I was locked in my own perceptual lens about *myself*. If we looked at our underlying operating systems, we could have, in the moment, discovered some interesting things:

Naomi: *I must deliver perfection (be perfect).*
Me: *I must deliver sophistication (be sophisticated).*

Both of these lenses created negative catabolic energy—Naomi in her own way, me in my own way. In order to shift these catabolic states, each of us would have had to have loosened up on our own lens. We would have had to have been open to the possibility of looking at the situation in some way other than a need to be perfect or sophisticated. If that was hard to do on our own, we might have been able to help each other see past our own lens, or we could have enlisted a trusted colleague to talk both of us through it. Who knows what actions or solutions might have been discovered? And who knows what *you* will discover for yourself, in your own situations?

Effective leadership requires you to engage the muscle of multiple perspectives in two different ways. One is how you work with other people to achieve better organizational outcomes. And the other is in how you work with yourself—how you self-manage—when you are triggered.

Let's look at four strategies to develop this muscle—strategies that apply no matter what the situation may be. They are:

1. Choosing curiosity over knowing
2. Loosening up your own lens
3. Discovering multiple lenses
4. Widening your lens beyond yourself

A quick caveat: Your underlying operating system does not really want you to read this section! Your underlying operating system specializes in single, narrow lenses designed to have you keep doing what you always done. I want you to be subversive. Read. Be open. Don't be ruled by your preprogrammed defaults.

This muscle will help you develop the ability to "see" your perceptual lens, in any given moment, for what it is: *one* of many possible ways to look at things. Why would you ever want to be limited to one perspective? That's being stuck. It restrains your leadership effectiveness and your quality of life. It limits you. Let's change that right now, by looking at the four strategies.

STRATEGY # 1: CHOOSE CURIOSITY OVER NEEDING TO BE RIGHT

Let's start with a thought experiment. I am going to have you experience two very different moods: *curiosity*, which creates value and effectiveness, and *needing to be right*, which destroys value and wreaks havoc. (It's your choice as to which one becomes your habit—and of course, I want you to choose curiosity/mental fitness!)

You're going to need your body for this experiment, so please sit up and uncross your arms and legs. Put your feet on the floor and sit upright but not rigid.

- First, just notice any body sensations that you may have (with this, you are practicing the muscle of self-assessment! See chapter 7).

No judgment, just notice.

- Think of a topic, person, or situation you are really curious to know more about. Or recall a recent time when you were really curious about something. (By doing this, you are creating a state or feeling of curiosity.)
- Stay in that state of curiosity for a little while. Pay attention to what's going through your body. You are trying to see what curiosity feels like. How would you describe it? In other words, how do you know that you are feeling or being curious right now? It's a different experience for everyone, so it's important for you to be able to recognize your own version of it.
- Now relax and stop. Don't overthink this.

What did you notice? Curiosity means having a strong desire to learn or know something. It is an *expansive* feeling. There is a sense of reaching outward—outside of yourself—toward the unknown. You want to know something that's new to you, to bring it into your own sphere of knowledge. When you are curious, you are in a state of "not-knowing-but-soon-will-learn." For the majority of people, this state feels really good.

Curiosity and the Bottom Line

Francesca Gino, a behavioral scientist and a professor at the Harvard Business School, laid out the business case for curiosity in a Harvard Business Review article a couple of years ago. Here's how her piece began: "Most of the breakthrough discoveries and remarkable inventions through history—from flint for starting a fire to self-driving cars—have something in common: They are the result of curiosity. The impulse to seek new information and experiences and explore novel possibilities is a basic human trait."

Professor Gino goes on to cite three business benefits that come from curiosity.

continued

1. Fewer decision-making errors. "When our curiosity is triggered, we are less likely to fall prey to confirmation bias, i.e., looking for information that supports our beliefs rather than for evidence that we are wrong."
2. "More innovation and positive changes in both creative and non-creative jobs."
3. Reduced group conflict. "Curiosity encourages members of a group to put themselves in one another's shoes and take an interest in one another's ideas, rather than focus on their own."

Now let's try the other mood, the state of "needing to be right." If you think this part of the exercise does not apply to you, then *surprise!* You are already in the state of needing to be right. Don't skip it. (By the way, when you have developed a high level of mental fitness, you will become very curious about your need to be right.)

As before, sit straight but not rigid, arms and legs uncrossed, feet flat on the floor.

- As a baseline, just notice any body sensations that you may have in this moment. No judgment, just notice.
- Think of a recent time when someone thought you were wrong, or strongly disagreed with your viewpoint, and you felt irritated, annoyed, defensive, or indignant. Recall how you tried to prove your point (or how you withdrew and then ruminated about it).
- Stay in that state of needing-to-be-right for a while. Pay attention to what it feels like in your body. How would you describe it?
- In other words, how do you know that you are needing to be right now? It's a different experience for everyone, so it's important for you to be able to recognize your own version of it.
- Relax and stop. Shake it off. You can now "dis-create" it by thinking other thoughts. (Great practice in shifting your mood!)

How you come to something—the mood with which you approach it—matters. *Really* matters. Look at some of the differences in outcomes when there is curiosity versus the need to be right:

CURIOSITY	THE NEED TO BE RIGHT
Expands possibilities	Shuts down possibilities
Draws ideas forth	Inhibits ideas
Uncovers, discovers data	Misses data (unseen, unheard)
Deepens relationships	Damages, hinders relationships
Heightens others' morale	Lowers others' morale
Opens dialogue	Shuts down communication

Choose curiosity as often as you can, in both leadership and life. When you find yourself needing to be right, practice shifting to curiosity. (You can always "go back" to your original position later, after you've heard other viewpoints or gained more data.) And yes: Sometimes you *are* right. Maybe even often. But this is not about whether you are right or wrong. It's about whether you are rigidly holding onto a *need* to be right—to feel right, to be seen as right, to be proclaimed by others as right. When you *need* to be right, you cannot engage productively with multiple perspectives.

One last point about this. Our discussion has been from the leader's perspective. But employing curiosity can also work as a way of pushing back against your boss when you think he is wrong. You might be tempted to say, "Boss, you have had tons of great ideas in the past, but this is not one of them." However, it can be so much more powerful if you restate his position to show you truly understand what he is advocating, and then say something like, "Tell me more. Why do you want to make this move? What are you seeing that I'm not seeing?"

With this approach, using curiosity, you're not attacking his ego in any way. You're saying, "I'm surprised that you're saying that. I'm seeing something else. Help me understand what you're seeing here." That opens up a dialogue for conversation.

It's the complete opposite of the stance "I'm right, you're wrong."

STRATEGY #2: LOOSEN UP YOUR OWN LENS

In mental fitness, you have to be able to loosen your perceptual lens so that you can "look" through other lenses that are offered by people with divergent perspectives. This is akin to suspending judgment, but taken to a whole new level. Here are some very common perceptual lenses that will need "loosening up" if you are to engage with other perspectives:

- I already know the solution
- I cannot lose, or, I will not let you win
- Only the data or facts matter

Other lenses related to your own ego or self-image are even harder to spot. Here are a few of them:

- This situation is about me
- I must have (or get) something (a raise; a promotion; $5 million) to be considered successful. (See sidebar.)
- This is "just how I am"
- I must be seen by others as … (smart, good, valuable, etc.)

The "I Must Have or Get Something" Lens

When I say that this lens—"I must have or get something"—needs loosening, I sometimes get pushback. "Wait, I am keeping my eye on the prize," people tell me. "The something—the promotion, raise, or whatever—is my motivation. Why is that bad?"

It doesn't have to be. It can be fine. It can be aspirational. But the point is, I don't want you to take the fact that you failed to make $5 million last year, or whatever your goal was, to mean you're a failure. True, you failed to reach that particular goal. But failing in one instance does not make you a failure overall.

Also, if you are too narrowly focused on the prize, the capacity for empathy or seeing things from others' perspectives sometimes gets lost.

At the highest executive levels, there is a particular situation I see all the time where these lenses play out. A leader—let's call her "Kay"—is part of a big organizational upheaval. Corporate functions are shifting, the org chart is changing, scopes of responsibility are being redistributed, and Kay hates what she sees and you can understand why. She's been told she's going to lose ten of her eighteen direct reports, as well as a substantial portion of her budget.

Kay has just spent the last two years working very diligently and strategically to acquire her turf—all those direct reports, a robust budget, and a fairly significant scope of influence. But now? Kay is angry. Worried. Disappointed. Confused. A large part of what she has worked so hard for is being taken away from her. How badly will this stall her career? How will she explain this apparent demotion on a resume? Why did this happen to her? What is everyone thinking about her now? Is she being forced out? Oh, and why did the company give Joe—that incompetent idiot—her best people, the ones she spent so much time mentoring and training?

I'm sure you can empathize with Kay. Maybe you've *been* Kay. It's not that Kay is wrong to have these thoughts. It's that she is stuck in one overarching and crushing perceptual lens: What is happening is bad for me.

To get unstuck, Kay needs to loosen up on this perceptual lens. There are other ways of looking at her situation. And indeed, she has to find some—like saying, "Okay, I hate this, but it's what is. I need to support the company's decision to the best of my ability, because this is what I am paid to do, but I also have to get my career back on track."

Using only one lens when presented with a troubling situation always limits your options.

But as long as she is in the grip of *this* negative lens—poor, poor pitiful me—she will not be able to engage with any other lenses or perspectives. When you engage with only one lens—as Kay is doing—you drastically limit yourself. You limit yourself: the possibilities you can consider, the moves you can make, how you show up as a leader. And ultimately, you limit the outcomes you can achieve.

To loosen up on your lens, you need to acknowledge that your lens is only one of multiple possible lenses. That's all you need to do. Just acknowledge that. *Believe* that. Make the habit of assuming there are always more ways to perceive, interpret, or understand a situation than your current way. It doesn't matter if you can't yet see other perspectives. Or you see them but you do not like them or want them. Just acknowledge that your lens is only one, not *the* one.

Now, I am not advocating Pollyanna thinking. If you flip your perceptual lens from "it's all bad" to "it's all good," then you will gain nothing. You will be just as stuck and in just as much pain—the pain and emotional drain of intense avoidance inherent in that thinking. And your leadership will be just as ineffective, just in other ways. Loosening the lens is about allowing a bit more of the unknown into your thinking.

Take a look at these examples, and try them out for yourself.

PERCEPTUAL LENS	THOUGHTS TO LOOSEN THE LENS
I already know the solution	What if... there is a better or another solution that has not yet been uncovered?
I cannot lose (or I will not lose)	What if ... there is something that needs to happen that is more important than winning and losing?
Only the data or facts matter	What if ... there are some intangibles that I have not yet accounted for?
This situation is about me	What if ... this situation has nothing to do with me?
I must have, or I must get (something)	What if ... I could let go of having to have or get, what would be possible then?
This is just how I am	What if ... I am "like this" only because I repeatedly tell myself a story about how I am "like this"?
I must be seen by others as ... (smart, good, valuable, etc.)	What if ... I could let go of being seen a certain way, since I can't control what others think anyway?

The questions in the right side of the table, the ones designed to loosen your lens, are not there to say your thinking was wrong. That wouldn't be productive! Instead, you are just asking, what else is there to see or understand here?

STRATEGY #3: DISCOVER MULTIPLE LENSES

Once you have created a mood of curiosity and you can acknowledge that your own perceptual lens is not *the* one, but rather *a* one, then you are well-positioned to discover additional lenses or perspectives. Like anything, learning to do this will take practice as you train yourself out of old habits. Here are two habits to start cultivating right away:

1. Ask open-ended questions rather than yes/no questions.
2. Listen carefully, rather than planning your response while someone else is talking. (Unfortunately, the old joke is true: Most people think the opposite of talking is "waiting for my turn to talk.")

Let's go over both points. Open-ended questions typically begin with words like *how, what, why,* and *tell me about.* They invite the other person to give a considered answer with some details and context instead of a simple yes or no. Once you've asked an effective question, make sure that you maintain your mood of curiosity while the other person answers. That puts you in the position to be listening carefully. Open-ended questions and engaged listening empower and encourage others. For example, direct reports and peers gain a chance to be heard, exercising their capacity to contribute. They feel appreciated. Taking this approach is a way to develop additional leaders.

I get that this can be challenging at times. Sometimes people don't express themselves clearly, or they speak reluctantly, or they ramble. You may find yourself bored or annoyed as they do. Maybe you just "know" that what the person is saying is off-topic, or not very useful. Oops! Without realizing it, you have just disengaged from curiosity. As the other person is still talking, and you are still looking at them, you are having a completely different conversation in your mind. You've slipped back into "knowing" and "needing to be right."

Start training yourself to listen longer. As soon as you notice that you slipped into "knowing," let it go. Come back to listening, to curiosity, to discovery. It could turn out that what is being said isn't terribly useful. But remember that engaging with multiple perspectives is not a linear, black-and-white process. You could hear just one phrase—or even one *word*—that becomes the catalyst for you to think about the topic in a whole new way. But if you're already preparing your dismissal of the person's perspective, or your defense of your own, that will never happen.

Change the Lens, Change the Outcome

Here's a common situation. You are going to a meeting called by your counterpart in a different department and you are not happy about it. The guy is a jerk, plain and simple. You are certain—because he has done it to you multiple times before—he is going to propose an initiative that will require your people to do most of the work, and for him to get most of the glory. You are strongly biased toward not trusting this leader.

All this may not even be conscious. But everything you hear during the meeting is going to be colored by your attitude, and it is going to color how you respond to him.

Now, he may very well be a jerk, and everything you feel may be true. But I would challenge how you approach him, and call upon you to change your lens—to step up and be a different kind of leader. How? By asking yourself, "How can I help this guy be a better leader? How can I align with this guy to make him more effective, in a way that doesn't make him feel small?"

It's a cliché because it is true: Be part of the solution, not part of the problem.

Triggers and Multiple Lenses

Open-ended questions and listening are invaluable when you find yourself emotionally triggered. A very powerful way to discover multiple lenses is to ask a trusted person (colleague, friend, coach, etc.) any of the following questions:

- What blind spots do I have right now that you can see, but that I am not seeing?
- What am I rejecting, shutting down, or defending against right now?
- What is a completely different perspective that I have not considered or am not allowing to be considered?

These open-ended questions are all ways of asking, "What am I missing?" It's about discerning what perceptual lens is active. When you are triggered, you are almost certainly missing something. That's because the fight-or-flight response naturally narrows your perspective and makes it laser-focused.

In this situation, it's most constructive to assume that you have blind spots and defenses going on. A trusted person with a different underlying operating system can likely articulate a very different perceptual lens—one that you would probably not think of on your own.

STRATEGY #4: WIDEN YOUR LENS BEYOND SELF

Let's return to Kay, the executive who just lost half of her direct reports in a company reorganization. She is reeling in anxiety. Her lens, or focus, is simple: What's happening is bad for me.

Kay's situation is extremely common. One day an executive is reporting to the CEO; the next day it's the COO or an EVP. Company reorganizations result in that happening all the time. Kay's response is typical, too. Her perspective is focused on herself. Leaders who put their own self-interest before those of their team or organization can be found everywhere. Most leaders start from this lens. They want to know, "What's in it for me? Is this good or bad for me?" Whatever is going on, they make it all about them, all about their future. Of course, the problem with that position is what is best for them may not be best for the organization—or their people.

Let's talk about the best way to handle this situation. First, there is dealing with the disruption. Then, we move on by laying out what you should do going forward.

Dealing with a Major Disruption to Your Status

Your company is restructuring and you're pissed off, because you don't like the impact on you. You're losing direct reports, budget, your title—or some combination of all three. In this kind of situation, it is very easy to become reactive and to fight to maintain what you had. It is much harder to step back and say, "Okay, this is tough. I know what I want, but are the moves they are making truly the right thing for the organization?" In other words, you have to put on a bigger lens and ask, "Why did they make this decision? How does this decision serve the organization? How might it be beneficial?"

From there, you take a somewhat smaller scope, and ask, "How does this affect my team? Is it better for them in the long run? Does it align us better in the organization?"

And only then do you finally get to ask, "What does all of this mean for me?"

Now, it's possible that you could go through the exercise and conclude you have been treated unfairly or that these changes really do not serve the organization, no matter what lens you apply. You might, in fact, decide you have to leave. That's fine. Just make sure that you don't damage your brand on the way out. The key point here: I want you to be a mature and resilient leader rather than reactive so that you can proceed forward powerfully, unencumbered by whatever has just happened, and recover quickly with resilience.

Moving on after Upheaval

Self-interest is the *worst possible lens*. I am well aware that many organizational changes seem not to be in a "demoted" executive's own best interest. But here's the key: I've seen leaders handle this change well—and I've seen them handle it poorly. The difference is whether or not the leader has mental fitness, and especially the ability to apply multiple lenses. The leader's success going forward is in direct proportion to their ability to adjust, be flexible, and deliver.

When these organizational upheavals occur, I coach the affected leaders to shift their lens. I have them engage with multiple lenses in the following way:

First lens: What's best for the organization?
Second lens: What's best for my team?
Last lens: What's best for me personally?

It's not an easy conversation. The affected leaders push back, hard. But I'm relentless on this point. I say to them: Look, you signed up for leadership. Big scope, big responsibility, big compensation. *How much of a leader* are you going to be right now? Are you going to whine and complain? Or step up?

What happened is "what is." It's reality. What opportunities can be found? While you act on behalf of your organization and your team, what can you (also) learn? How can you grow? For example: What will you learn about being put into a situation when you think that situation is the worst for you? How will you deal with your limiting belief system that says you have just been screwed? Learning from this is an important part of your leadership task. It is part of your job.

It is a big leap to shift from the lens of self to the lens of organization and team—but it's not impossible. You have to be willing to engage with multiple lenses. If you do, this shift leads to completely different ideas and actions. The leaders who are successful are able to adjust. They can wrap their arms around the organization changes, and whether or not they agree with them, they can get on board in order to realize the benefits to the company and/or their team.

In this light, with the lens shift in place, what does "success" look like for this leader? If the executive aligns her actions with the organization's and team's interests rather than prioritizing her own personal interests, the people above her on the org chart see her clear commitment. They see mental fitness in action. They become her strong, deep allies. It's like money in the bank—a relationship investment, if you will. The executive is viewed by the top as being more valuable to the organization, because she is aligned with its interests. She is now well-positioned for any additional shake-up or other change.

Perhaps you are finding this version of "success" hard to imagine. Then consider the opposite: a demoted leader who sulks, opposes, stonewalls, sabotages, or withdraws. That's a leader who accomplishes nothing for the organization (or worse, hinders its progress) because she is so focused on her own agenda. Do you think that's a better outcome? It's no leap to guess what happens to *that* leader.

I am advocating taking a very large, wide perspective and employing a growth mindset, always seeking the bigger picture. Understand that it's not just *you* in the picture. Learn to quickly reframe. For example, you could first shift from a lens of *yourself* to a lens of *others in the company*. Then shift from a lens of others to the lens of the *overall company*. Then go even bigger— beyond the organization. At that point, your perspective becomes inclusive and holistic: self, others, team, organization, community, the world. Look at how many possibilities open up when you can engage with *all* of these multiple perspectives.

This takes practice, but it's just a muscle like all of the others we've talked about. Pay attention, commit to it, and train yourself day by day. I assure you that once you experience the possibilities that open up by using it, you'll rarely (if ever) go back to that limited "self" lens again.

Think bigger than yourself and your self-interests. Doing so is almost always great leadership.

POTENTIAL ROAD BUMP #1: YOU ARE OVERPLAYING THIS MUSCLE

There's an important caveat about engaging with multiple lenses. When you overuse this muscle, it becomes counterproductive and causes a whole different set of leadership inefficiencies. I see this problem often at the top of organizations. Some leaders take multiple perspectives to a harmful extreme.

Here's an example of what happens. An executive patiently listens to all sides. He actively encourages inclusion and divergent opinions. Everyone feels heard. But there is an unacknowledged dark side to this executive's behavior. Internally, he wants everyone to feel good. He is uncomfortable with conflict and confrontation. He lingers in the stage of asking questions instead of putting a stake in the ground and making a decision. Why? Since his decision cannot please everyone, some people will be upset by the road he chooses to go down; he sees that as conflict. He does not want to deal with it.

This leader cannot powerfully drive results. He stalls decisions. He pushes issues back to his team members to work things out themselves, avoiding the need to take a stand. Other leaders, below him, try to make things move forward but become frustrated. They start working around this leadership void.

The overplayed muscle is especially evident when an organizational redesign negatively impacts employees. This leader will be required to hold crucial conversations with the affected employees—regarding position changes, process changes, scope changes, and so on. Conflict-averse as this leader is, he will be slower than his peers to hold those talks. His foot-dragging will be very apparent and seen as inefficiency and weakness.

My caveat to leaders is to use this muscle judiciously. Multiple perspectives are important, but you must also be able to move decisions forward. If you're not sure if you're overplaying this muscle, take a look at the items below. Generally speaking, which apply to you?

- You are a natural helper or caretaker
- You dislike conflict or confrontation
- You do not want to hurt anyone's feelings
- You are good at harmonizing groups or teams
- You are naturally empathetic
- You place others' needs before your own
- You do not like highly assertive communication styles
- You have a belief that it will all work out—resolve itself—without the need for your intervention

The more of the above that apply to you, the more likely you are overusing the muscle. Your underlying operating system wants to please others. You are overly concerned with not making waves, being accommodating, fair and egalitarian, treating people well, and so on. It's not that all of this is bad. But as with all lenses, make sure you are actually aware and choosing to use it when appropriate. Don't let it be an overused, counterproductive default pattern.

POTENTIAL ROAD BUMP #2: YOU *STILL* NEED TO BE RIGHT

Please hear me on this. You do not *need* to always be right. You only *think* you need to be right.

I know I have already said this. But I cannot emphasize this point enough. In fact, I could fill the whole book on this topic alone. When you are a leader who has to be right, you cause some of the greatest damage possible to both your teams and organization. Your behavior is defensive. It shuts down people, possibilities, and progress. It's like knocking a wheel off a running race car, or pulling tracks off a railroad when a train approaches at high speed. It is incredibly derailing. The damage is not easily repaired, and it is extremely costly.

The need to be right is not about actually *being* right. It is really about protecting your "self." You are strongly attached to the way that you think about yourself, and this attachment shows up in your language and behavior as defensiveness. You are driven to maintain the image or belief that you have about yourself. So, you defend. And defend. And defend some more. You defend as strongly as you possibly can against any perspective that does not align with your version of your self.

I get that you are smart. It's even very likely that you are truly the smartest person in the room. But for all your capability, you are also completely unaware of your own rigidity and ego-protecting defense mechanisms. When you are driven by this need to be right, you are operating with the narrowest of perceptual lenses. Not only are you making every situation about you, but you're making it about your own internal insecurities. Your defenses even prevent you from being aware of these insecurities. But that doesn't make them any less responsible for your behavior. (All of this is the stuff of the unseen underlying operating system.)

Yes, people will want you around for your intelligence, or innovative thinking, or problem-solving, and whatever else you bring to the table. They may even laud you for your contributions. *But not indefinitely.* Sooner or later, your defenses—your inability to allow multiple perspectives—will cause significant problems. It is simply not sustainable in the long run. Once you are seen as hindering organizational progress, other leaders will start working around you. The wider organization will move toward managing you out. Your reputation will precede you in the wider marketplace.

If this is you, please revisit the strategies described in this chapter. Start small as you begin to try them out. Experiment with them in low-stakes situations where you already feel less need to defend. Notice the results. How do people react to your different behaviors? What are the outcomes of your conversations or meetings? How are they different; improved? As you develop more capacity and confidence using this muscle, continue to increase your use in more settings with higher stakes. Allow a "need to be curious" to become your new way of being.

Key Points

- **Effective leadership** requires you to engage the muscle of multiple perspectives in two different ways: with the people you work with, and how you think when you are triggered.
- **Four strategies to develop this muscle**:
- Choose curiosity over knowing.
- Loosen up your own lens.
- Discover multiple lenses.
- Widen your lens beyond yourself.
- **When organizational upheavals occur**, and they will, engage your lens in this order:
- **First lens:** What's best for the organization?
- **Second lens:** What's best for my team?
- **Last lens:** What's best for me personally?

  Yes, this is difficult, but it exemplifies a mature leader.

- **There is always another point of view.** Always remember there could be other perspectives than your own.
- Remember **the lens you use affects what you see—and what you don't—as well as how you respond.** That's why you want to employ multiple lenses.

9

CALMING YOUR PHYSIOLOGY

Q: What does my physical body have to do with leading lightly?

A: Calming your physiology is essential for leading lightly. Think about any of the common physiological manifestations of catabolic energy, such as a knot in the stomach, shallow or rapid breathing, and tense muscles. How can your body be light in these states? It can't, and that is by design. In a catabolic state, our physiology and energy state are concentrated in order to be laser-focused on fighting against that perceived threat.

Leading lightly is an expansive state, not a contracted one. It's a state in which we are open; we see more perspectives, see more options or possibilities. The body is at ease. That doesn't mean there is no effort, but the body is performing, not contracting. Think of an athlete executing their skill. They practice their physical movements when they are not under "threat" or competition, and then in the moment it's necessary they move with speed, elegance, and skill. There is no fear or pain involved. Likewise, developing your muscles for deep breathing now can later help get you out of a triggered state quickly so that you can lead lightly.

The muscle to rapidly modulate your own physiology is used to interrupt your body's fight-or-flight stress response and quickly return to a relaxed state.

Every day we see headlines about exciting new technologies, new inventions, and new twists on old ideas. Start-ups seek to disrupt everything—in business and our personal lives—with their innovations. Tech giants seek to sell massive quantities of new products, features, updates. And thought leaders seek to instill deep clarity on the ethics, usage, and legalities of it all.

Well, I'd like to introduce you to an absolutely *brilliant* idea that hasn't gotten a lot of press, but its benefits are almost too good to be true. When used correctly, it helps you think more clearly, feel more energized, and be more effective, and it generates greater health and well-being. At the same time, it will reduce your negative, unproductive emotions such as anger, anxiety, and feeling overwhelmed. What is that miraculous thing?

Breathing.

Oh, sorry, were you expecting something more exciting?

I've given you this big buildup because I'd like you to think about breathing differently than you ever have. It's not that what I have to tell you about breathing is new. The benefits and methods have been studied, written about, and taught for years, in many different ways, cultures, and contexts.

Breathing, done correctly, will make you a better person—and a better leader.

In executive circles, the value of paying attention to your breathing is often discounted—or ignored. It can be viewed as too fluffy or too spiritual, or it's just too *simple*. As a result, the relationship of breathing to effective corporate leadership is often overlooked and underestimated. That's a huge mistake.

As you know by now, mental fitness is all about minimizing fight-or-flight responses and keeping your body, mind, and energy in a predominantly anabolic or restorative state. Most of our mental fitness muscles are focused around choices and skills in the mental domain, but this particular muscle is different; it's actually in the body. The reality is that you are not just a discombobulated head floating around thinking and talking. Your body is always there too, and your catabolic or negative responses occur throughout the body. We can't leave the body out of our understanding of mental fitness.

So, one of the core muscles of mental fitness is a physical skill that you will use in concert with the other muscles we have discussed. Specifically, it is the skill to change, or modulate, your own body out of a triggered state—*rapidly*. There is little use or effectiveness in taking hours or days to calm your body after an emotional upset! Yet for most people who have been strongly triggered, that long timeframe is the norm. Think back to our discussion about Joe in chapter 4. He remained in a triggered state for *five days* after an unsettling run-in with his boss.

In the heat of anger, or at the height of anxiety, or in the turmoil of frustration, the most direct and accessible way to modulate your body's triggered state is to breathe in a particular and deliberate way called "diaphragmatic breathing," or deep abdominal breathing. We'll look at the mechanics of it in a moment, but for now, think of this form of breathing as your own personal technology for critical oxygen delivery and replenishment.

What Is Diaphragmatic Breathing?

The Cleveland Clinic describes it well: "Diaphragmatic breathing is intended to help you use the diaphragm correctly while breathing to:

- Strengthen the diaphragm
- Decrease the work of breathing by slowing your breathing rate
- Decrease oxygen demand
- Use less effort and energy to breathe"*

* https://my.clevelandclinic.org/health/articles/9445-diaphragmatic-breathing

When you are in a strongly catabolic state, your breathing defaults to short, shallow breaths. Your lens—your vision and attention—narrows so that you can focus solely on the perceived danger that has triggered the rapid breathing. You have a heightened awareness of the danger—but limited awareness of everything else around you. It's as if nothing else exists.

But as an executive facing a difficult situation or experiencing an emotional trigger, what you actually *need* is a strong supply of oxygen to your brain. You need clarity and calm; you need to be centered and present. Diaphragmatic breathing does at least two critical things for you: it oxygenates you in the full and replenishing way that you need, and it sends clear signals to your body's nervous system that "everything is okay. There is no real danger here."

WHY DIAPHRAGMATIC BREATHING IS SO IMPORTANT

How long does it typically take to calm yourself down after you've been angry, panicked, frustrated, overwhelmed, or otherwise upset? Consider your own patterns. As you do, also consider the techniques you generally use to reset yourself, to calm down, to feel better. Is it venting to others? Listening to music? Doing yoga or meditating? Distracting yourself with TV? Turning to alcohol or other substances? Or perhaps simply waiting for time to pass?

If you are developing your mental fitness, then none of these strategies are your best bet for *in-the-moment correction*. Either they're not healthy options, or they require a lot of logistics or time. Focus on rapid speed of physiological recovery. Your new metric is going to be *time*. With mental fitness, we seek to measure the recovery of your body in just seconds to minutes. When you use diaphragmatic breathing correctly, you will drastically reduce your recovery time.

HOW TO MODULATE YOUR PHYSIOLOGY

This strategy for modulating your physiology is not the only one that exists, but it's one that is easy to learn and apply, and extraordinarily effective. As we go along, you won't just be reading; I'm going to ask you to actually try the strategy as well. One note, before we begin: as in all things, the mindset that you bring to this is going to either help you or hinder you. Please watch yourself for these common impeding beliefs:

- This is too simple. It can't have any real impact.
- I know how to breathe. I don't need to be told.
- I'll wait and do this later when I actually need it.

You will learn the utility and benefits of this strategy only by trying it and practicing it. It only takes a few minutes a day, and you can do it anywhere, at any time. I can't think of any excuses or rationalizations for skipping it that I would possibly accept! In order for you to be proficient with this skill when it is needed—when you are triggered—you must first become fluent by practicing it under relaxed conditions. Just think of how athletes train: they don't practice only when in the midst of a real game or high-stakes competition! Nor should you.

Stop and Oxygenate

When you are in a deeply triggered emotional state, you won't be able to think your way out of it. In fact, you can't think very much at all! When you find yourself in this state, you need to *stop* and then *oxygenate*. This strategy creates a critical pause that prevents you from doing something really stupid (and likely regrettable; see sidebar) in your nonthinking reactive state. And it will help you oxygenate your brain so you can regain your ability to think more productively about what's happening.

Eliminating the Regrets That Come with Not Breathing

Here is a classic example of what happens if you don't breathe when you are under stress. It's classic because just about everyone has experienced it.

You get an email and you are instantly pissed. Your reaction: "You have to be effing kidding me!" Whatever the email said, you have just been triggered. You grab your keyboard or phone. You furiously start typing—or tapping, or

continued

indignantly dictating—your response. With a final emphatic thump, you hit SEND.

A couple of minutes later, you realize what you've just done. Now comes the regret: "OMG, I am an idiot. I never should have responded that way!" You desperately Google "how to recall a sent email" . . . and find that nothing will work—the message has already been read.

This situation is the exact one in which you should have started breathing and looking at things from another perspective. Sure, you might still write the email, but you likely wouldn't send it. You would just get the initial catabolic thoughts out of your system. Then, you could have proceeded more constructively.

First, STOP

As soon as you are aware that you are triggered, reactive, or upset, STOP. Stop whatever you are saying or doing. Yes, it's that simple, but you'd be surprised at how many people don't fully grasp what I'm saying. I mean:

- If you are engaged with others, STOP talking—or yelling or defending or complaining. Stop in mid-sentence, if that's what you have to do!
- If you are in the midst of writing an angry, defensive, or accusatory email, STOP your hands and fingers from moving. Push yourself away from the keyboard.
- If you're indulging in silent rumination about how awful everything is, tell yourself to STOP this right now! If you're sitting, stand up. If you're standing, sit down. Stop the rumination.

Then, Oxygenate

Here are the steps. Please read them first. Then read them a second time, and actually do the steps as you go along.

1. Take in a big, deep breath. Make sure your belly is getting bigger. If your chest is getting bigger and your belly smaller you are doing it incorrectly.
2. Hold it while you silently count six seconds.

3. Release the breath slowly.
4. Repeat as needed.

When you are counting six seconds, make sure to say to yourself, "One one-hundred, two one-hundred, three one-hundred" all the way up to six. That will ensure that you don't shortchange the full six seconds. If it's easier, look at the second hand on your watch, or use a timer on your smartphone. You'll be tempted to simply estimate or to think, "One, two, three . . ." but don't do that. When you shortchange yourself, the exercise will not be effective.

This method of oxygenation is the fastest way to physiologically get your body out of a triggered state. If a true threat were really happening to you, you would not be able to physically make your muscles breathe this way. A true emergency is a survival issue, and your breathing would remain shallow and rapid.

Use SOS

When you are triggered, don't react. Instead, remember and execute this quick phrase: SOS.

Stop. **O**xygenate. **S**eek new information.

The SOS technique combines three of the mental fitness muscles in quick succession.

1. To Stop, you must be aware that you've been triggered. That in-the-moment awareness comes from developing the muscle to self-assess your internal state (chapter 7).
2. To Oxygenate, you use the muscle to modulate your physiology (the subject of this chapter). In other words, you breathe, hold, and exhale to signal "safety" to your brain. You do this with depth and intention.
3. To Seek new information, you use the muscle to engage with multiple perceptual lenses (chapter 8). You realize that the way you're currently seeing your situation is unnecessarily narrowed by the sense of threat, and that it's only one of many ways to see

things. You seek new data, information, or perspectives to try to shift your lens. You do this by consciously reaching for other lenses that you know of but aren't using at that moment, you talk to a trusted person, or you request some feedback or other information to change your point of view. Your new lens or lenses then open up new possibilities for your response.

When you oxygenate with these deep breaths that you hold for six seconds, you are essentially tricking your physiology. You're giving your body signals in a language that it understands that *there is no threat here.*

Please go through the steps of oxygenation one more time (deep breath, hold for six seconds, release slowly). When you take your deep breath, just do the best you can. Notice how it feels. Easy? Awkward? Tight and uncomfortable? Don't worry about whether it feels good or not. It is going to be effective either way.

Practice Makes Normal

Most of us have a habit of shallow breathing, and so the muscles involved (chest, diaphragm, etc.) may have limited range of motion. If they do, when you take that deeper breath, it may feel strained. For now, that's okay. Later, when you have learned diaphragmatic breathing, you will take your deep breaths using that musculature. But, first things first! Practice the oxygenation strategy several times a day (when you are not particularly stressed out) to get the rhythm and feel of it. And start trying it when you're under pressure or triggered, too.

I encourage you to practice changing your breathing at a fundamental level so that it becomes your new norm. Although I'm teaching diaphragmatic breathing for your self-management, in reality it is just normal, healthy breathing using your body's anatomy as designed! Way back when, when you took your first breath as a newborn baby—and as a growing infant—you naturally used diaphragmatic breathing. It is only over time, as the stresses and anxieties of life built up and you started living in an ongoing catabolic state, that your breathing habits changed.

When you have a habit of shallow breathing, you use your chest muscles and rib cage to pull air in and out. The space you can fill with air is limited. Your shoulders and neck will often be tight. It's just not something that most of us have any real awareness about until we actually try to breathe more deeply.

Hyperventilating

Can this deep breathing lead to hyperventilating?

The answer is no. You can't possibly hyperventilate because hyperventilating is shallow, rapid breathing. What we are talking about here is deep, slow breathing. It's the opposite of hyperventilation.

The diaphragm is the muscle whose shape, strength, and position are designed to help you efficiently inhale and exhale large amounts of air. It is a dome-shaped sheet of muscle and tendons that contracts to move down and expand the chest cavity when you breathe in, and rises as it relaxes when you exhale. It's the muscle that causes the movement of your belly out and in as you breathe.

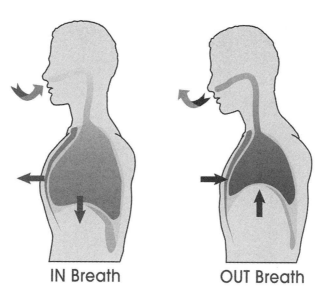

IN Breath   OUT Breath

Try this: put your hand on your stomach right now, near your belly button. Simply breathe without changing anything and notice the movement of your hand. At this stage it's helpful just to have awareness of that movement. If your diaphragm muscle is tight, it may take some time to loosen it up. Work on it each day; hand on your belly, simply breathing. Deepen your breath as you are able. Maintain that deeper breathing for a minute or so. Gradually increase the time to several minutes, and more. If music helps you relax, go ahead and use it. The key is to encourage your diaphragm muscle to contract further to expand your lungs more as you focus on deepening the inhale and exhale of your breath.

ROAD BUMPS TO MODULATING PHYSIOLOGY

In some ways, this mental fitness muscle—modulating your physiology with correct breathing—is the most straightforward of all the muscles. But despite this being a physical skill, the majority of the road bumps that you may encounter are going to relate to your mindset, attitude, or beliefs.

Do any of these describe you?

- You skimmed this chapter. We're lucky you're reading even this sentence!
- You did not try the breathing exercises along with the descriptions. You simply read through them and would like to move on now.
- You did try them, and don't plan to practice further because you don't want to or don't need to.
- You tried, but physically could not take a deep breath. If so, you have already hit a road bump! Read on.

POTENTIAL ROAD BUMP #1:
SUBSTITUTING OTHER RELAXATION TECHNIQUES

If you have regularly practice yoga or meditation, get massages, or use aromatherapy or music to calm yourself, you may be wondering why that isn't good enough. Do you still need to practice the six-second oxygenation and the diaphragmatic breathing?

Yes, you do, and here's why. Executive leaders are very busy and routinely face highly stressful situations. If this describes you, you want the most effective and *efficient* means available for the moment. There are times when you are going to be triggered. You're human! It's going to happen! You will need an effective strategy to *rapidly* shift in that moment. For example, if your boss is angrily in your face or you are in a contentious meeting with a whole bunch of angry people you need a method that you can do right then and there.

When you are in the heat of action, in battle, you will want you to recover and adapt with agility. And I want you to respond to that next moment with your fullest performance capacity! Oxygenation and diaphragmatic breathing can be done quickly right where you are, without anyone noticing what you are doing. Frankly, with everything moving fast around you, you don't have time to do anything else.

Breathing helps you gain capacity and perspective. It allows you to look at things differently and optimize your performance.

In mental fitness, we are training your body to get out of its triggered state very quickly. I care about the speed of this shift, and I want you to care about it too. We want to get the body out of the catabolic state as fast as possible and stay out of that state. Other practices may calm your system, but they generally take twenty minutes or more. In addition, many of these practices require particular logistics or space to do them in (such as yoga, massage, exercise). If you are in a deeply catabolic state at work, with people all around you, then obviously you are not going to do any of these other practices in that moment, in that setting.

There can also be a false sense of "okay-ness" when using these practices. Perhaps you have done a yoga session, or you listened to relaxing music for a while, or you took a walk to cool down, and now you "feel better." This does not necessarily mean you have permanently shifted out of your catabolic state. To be clear, I very much believe in the value of the many diverse and available practices that serve to calm, ground, and relax the mind and body. In fact, I often recommend various approaches to clients based on their goals. But while doing these practices regularly and with intention can help you to generally remain calmer and more anabolic throughout each day, they are not a *substitute* for the oxygenation and diaphragmatic breathing.

Finally, if you are someone who already does breathing practices such as pranayama, ujjayi breath, breath counting, 4-7-8, or any other of the many wonderful, valuable practices out there, please know that the oxygenation and diaphragmatic breathing are distinct from what you are doing, and need to be practiced in their own right. Each has its own benefits.

Remember, mental fitness is about a *rapid* shift. And of all the techniques out there, diaphragmatic breathing is the one most capable of shifting your mood quickly.

POTENTIAL ROAD BUMP #2: YOU ARE ALREADY SO CHILL, YOU DON'T NEED THIS

One of the hardest things about explaining this road bump is actually getting the attention of the people to whom it applies! So let's try another checklist. Take a look and see if any apply to you.

- You think of yourself as pretty chill, not too many emotional ups and downs.
- You might be annoyed or quite upset inside, but you hide it well on the outside.
- You let everything slide off your back because things just aren't that important anyway.
- You have a favorite catch phrase that makes you feel better about everything, such as "It's all good," or "I got this."

If any of these apply to you, then your road bump is going to be a failure to recognize or acknowledge when you are triggered. You will be blind to it. You will not realize that you actually need to oxygenate in that moment. For you, the catabolic state is often "slippery." You have developed a coping mechanism of denial in order not to feel the discomfort or inconvenience of strong negative feelings. When unwanted things happen, you just tell yourself (and others), "It's fine, it's no big deal." You don't acknowledge that you really are bothered. For example, those cute little catch phrases like "it's all good" are simply lullabies. They soothe your feelings so that you can avoid digging beneath the surface to get at the root of the problem. Maybe you know there actually is a problem—you are aware on some level—but you try to ignore it to make it go away.

If you were in a coaching session with me, I would strongly challenge your habit of minimizing, denying, or ignoring any of these feelings. Your method of dealing with them is a form of flight, but it is not obvious in the way that literally running away would be. This is much more subtle—slippery, as I said—and therefore so much harder for you to catch. If this is your habit, it's likely that even now, as you read this, you're denying that you engage with problems in this way.

This is not something that can be overcome by reading a book, but what I would say to you is practice the oxygenation and diaphragmatic breathing anyway—whether you think you need it or not. Do not rely on your assessment that you've already got this and have no need because you don't get upset. You *do* get upset, and you do need to shift yourself out of it. Not in the false denying way, but in the real physiological way. Practice the strategies!

POTENTIAL ROAD BUMP #3: YOU CAN'T TAKE A DEEP BREATH

Sometimes I encounter a client who cannot take a deep breath. Their body is so tight—they hold so much chronic tension—that their muscles, tissues, and bones cannot expand and contract enough to make space for more air to come in and out. The ribs do not move; the chest does not flex; the diaphragm is locked in place. Trying to breathe more deeply is uncomfortable at best, and painful at worst. The inability to take that breath can increase frustration, as well.

This type of client has often had significant trauma in their life. They are deeply distrustful of people and of life in general, and they go through every day in a hyperaware, hypervigilant state. It's as if they are in a self-imposed prison, living under continual threat. They hold themselves very rigidly as a form of self-protection. When someone has this kind of extreme, chronic tension in the body, then the mental fitness breathing exercises will not be particularly effective. These individuals need a much more nuanced and holistic approach to working with their physiology in order to break up the deep tissue tension.

There are a lot of things that can be done to help this process along, such as deep tissue massage, Rolfing, guided meditations, and visualizations. At times, I have recommended these types of methods to executive clients to help them get more quickly to the state where their muscles can support deeper breathing and oxygenation. When their bodies have more mobility, they can get the benefits of the breathing approaches we have talked about here, and are more able to rapidly shift in moments of trigger.

Key Points

- When used correctly, **breathing can help you think** more clearly, feel more energized, and be more effective in your interactions.
- **Breathing reduces your negative, unproductive feelings** such as anger and anxiety.
- There are many techniques that will calm your body. But **diaphragmatic breathing is the most direct** and accessible way to modulate your body's triggered state.
- **Employing effective breathing is a two-step process**. First, STOP whenever you are doing that has put you in a triggered state, and then take in a breath and hold it for a full six seconds.
- This method of **oxygenation is the fastest way** to physiologically get your body out of a triggered state.

10

HOW TO PERFORM AT YOUR BEST AND CHANGE YOUR BRAIN

Q: When will I truly be leading lightly?

A: The goal of changing your brain is to make leading lightly your new normal. It becomes your default and not an occasional thing or a technique to apply.

Each old pattern that you release or change; each old assumption that you release or change; each customary judgment that you release or change helps alter your brain. And that holds true for each new perspective that you adopt. At some point, the rewiring is complete enough that your brain defaults now to leading lightly instead of the old way. You'll always be fine-tuning, but you've got the major pieces in place for leading lightly to be your new way of being in the world.

———

Picture this: You're at work. It's been a tough week. In fact, it's been a brutal quarter. A long-simmering issue has just come to a head. You're in an all-hands-on-deck executive meeting, hastily called to deal with this crisis.

*You perform at your best when you rapidly
transform your negative mood or physiological
state into a more neutral or relaxed state as soon
as it starts by simultaneously applying all five
muscles of mental fitness.*

The situation is challenging. Tempers are flaring. There's lots of blame and finger-pointing going around, and no one is taking responsibility. Because the department you lead is at the heart of the crisis, all eyes are now on *you*. Everyone is waiting: What are you going to say or do next? How are you, *the leader*, going to respond?

Before we decide, let's understand the specifics of the situation you are facing.

You're working for a young company focused on growth and scaling aggressively. And you, the head of sales, have just found out in this hastily called meeting that the company is going to miss its quarterly projections, by a lot, at a time when your organization is about to go out for another round of funding. Everyone from the board of directors on down is stressed by this surprising and potentially extremely damaging fact.

The CEO turns to you and with no preamble says, "What the hell happened? We're missing our revenue forecast by 12 percent because our best salesman walked before closing the deals we were counting on. He reported directly to you and you didn't see this coming? How did this happen?" This is what you're up against. Some people have seen you in a crisis situation before. They think they know you and how you'll respond. Others are newer; they don't know what will happen.

You can hear the proverbial pin drop in the room.

How you respond next is critical. It is the very definition of *performance*. You know it's a make-or-break moment. You want to rise to the occasion; you want to shine. But inside? You're not shining. You're anxious. Confused. You try to think—but you can't. You are emotionally *triggered*.

If you are like most of us, what triggers you is that unexpected moment when someone says something to you. Implies something. Undermines you. Throws you under the bus. It can be anything, or everything. It can be real. It can be imagined. In our scenario here, it's a little bit of everything with lots of people indicating that this is all your fault. The immediate cause of your trigger doesn't actually matter, however, because whatever it was, that's not what your real problem is now. Your real problem is that you are emotionally triggered in a key moment when you need to be demonstrating optimal performance.

But while that is the problem, your *perceptual lens* leads you to believe that you, personally, are under a threat of some kind. The fight-or-flight lens has kicked in! The company just lost its superstar closer; worse, it's going to miss the financial projections it promised investors. And the CEO is right about this: You are directly responsible.

What do you do next?

The old you—before mental fitness—would have been predictable. Anyone who knew you would have been able to guess how you would respond; they would have seen your typical reaction many times before. You would have followed your usual pattern. Maybe defensive, maybe shutting down. Maybe angry, maybe sullen. Maybe terse. At best, it would have been unproductive. At worst, destructive. And all of it would have been purely reactive, driven by that emotional trigger.

In the past, you would have felt anxious and threatened, and you would have responded aggressively. You would probably have said something like: "Everyone is glossing over one important detail. True, the salesman was going to be responsible for delivering 12 percent of the expected revenues. [*And when he did, you were going to feel like a hero, since you helped him identify the key clients to target.*] And true, the two of us didn't always get along. But that wasn't the reason he left. The fact of the matter was he got a dramatically better offer from someone outside the industry—twice the base salary and twice the commission rate."

But the people in the meeting don't know that—and quite frankly they don't care. Especially the CEO! And then you might have counterattacked:

"What the hell did you want me to do? We couldn't come anywhere near to matching the offer."

Or maybe you would try to minimize the loss and tell the group: "We really don't need the guy. There are sales in the pipeline. We can do it. It will just take a little longer than we expected."

All of that is what you would have probably done before developing your mental fitness. But this time, it's different.

This time, you don't do that habitual thing. In this critical moment, you use all of the mental fitness muscles—together, seamlessly—to make a dramatic internal shift. In fact, you shift yourself right out of the emotionally triggered state and into optimal leadership performance. You do it so fast that no one notices.

As a result of everything you have been learning, you are not going to be defensive, not going to blow up, not going to feel overly threatened—and even if you feel yourself slipping, you are going to shift out of it quickly. And when you do, you will be more effective and say things like this: "Okay. Here's where we are. Our best salesman is gone. We can't change that. We need to accept what is. What we need now is all hands on deck. And here's the strategy for doing that. Everyone who can will help with sales. For example, this is now a hands-on part of *my* job.

"And Mr. CEO, I am going to bring you in at the end to help close the deals that the departing salesman had in the pipeline, and hopefully by the time you have done that, we will have also generated a few more for you to bring to a successful conclusion. Having you involved shows these potential clients that they are important to us, and it will allow us to move faster—since we won't have to take deals to you for your approval—and it doesn't hurt that you are very good at sales.

"This strategy will allow us to close that 12 percent gap. And if we can't close it completely, we will be in a far better position to outperform the projections for the next quarter, which will allow us to get our momentum back. And while all this is going on, I am going to be working with a leading search firm to find not one, but two superstar salespeople so we can avoid this situation in the future."

With this shift, you write a different ending. A much better ending. *You perform at your best.*

How is this possible? Because you have practiced and developed the five muscles of mental fitness: self-assessing your internal state, embodying personal accountability, choosing a helpful lens, holding multiple perspectives, and moderating your physiology. With intent, focus, and commitment, you have worked each muscle separately, like an athlete who goes to the gym and hits the weight machines, working your biceps, pecs, and quads each in turn.

In this, your big moment, all your mental fitness muscles come together. You aren't thinking or analyzing. There is no time for that! A championship basketball player at the free throw line is not thinking about his triceps. A pro tennis player serving a match point is not thinking about her quads. And when *you* need to perform—in your leadership role, like now with people freaking out about the potential loss in sales—you do not think about which mental fitness muscles you're using. You're the mental athlete, coordinating all your available muscles with speed and precision.

In this chapter, we are going to see how all the mental fitness muscles work together as you create that all-important shift out of an emotionally triggered state. As you read, please note that it may seem like the process is linear, i.e., step-by-step. In reality, it's not; it happens quickly, organically, and slightly differently for each individual. However, we have to break it down for the sake of learning. So think of this as a slow-motion demonstration. And indeed, you will practice in this kind of slow-motion way as you learn to coordinate all the muscles together. Once you've mastered each individual skill and thought pattern, the coordination will happen in real time.

THE PLAYING FIELD

Physical fitness is easy to observe. You can see the body, the muscles, the performance. In fact, if you are at a sporting event, a big part of the excitement is being able to observe athleticism in action. We talk about those great plays for days. *Touchdown! Home run! Game, set, match! A new world record!*

But what about mental fitness? What about performance, when performance means rapidly shifting out of an emotionally triggered state—or never getting triggered in the first place? As outsiders, we cannot see most of the mental fitness on the "playing field," i.e., when the shift occurs, because it's *within* you.

If a colleague happens to be in the room with you when it happens, at first he may see some external sign of negative emotion in your body language or physiology. But as you actually engage in making the shift, there is very little that is externally visible for him to observe. He *might* see the following:

- You take a breath and hold it for six seconds.
- You pause (and appear to be thinking).
- Your face or body seems to relax into a more neutral or positive state.
- You constructively engage with whatever is going on.

As seen from the outside, that's about it. There's no external drama. Nothing obvious happens. There is just a shift of energy and the ability to move forward in a constructive way.

THE SHIFT ON THE INSIDE

With so little to see on the outside, what's happening on the inside? Remember earlier on, we pretended to have a special MindMastery camera, the one that could see and record thoughts and mood? Let's use it again to "see" all the muscles of mental fitness in action as you are shifting out of being triggered. When we play back the recording in slow motion, we would see you do the following:

- **Assess** your mood and notice that you are emotionally triggered.
- **Breathe** in and hold it for six seconds to calm your physiology.
- **Choose to take accountability** for shifting your mood.
- **Spot your own perceptual lens** by recognizing your thoughts and identifying the core thought driving your reaction.
- **Explore alternative lenses** and thoughts.
- **Elect a more helpful lens** (and thoughts) that empower, rather than impede you.

You may think that six steps are a lot to remember, but I'm going to give you two easy ways to recall these steps as you first start practicing shifting out of a triggered state. I promise it will be as easy as **ABC (SEE)**!

Steady Yourself. Then Change Your Lens.

Triggered states make you emotionally off-balance inside. Steadying yourself is the most basic, most fundamental thing you need to do to respond optimally.

When you are emotionally triggered, you cannot think clearly, if you are able to think at all. To shift into performance, you will need to

1) Steady yourself, and
2) Change your lens.

Because it's so hard to think under those circumstances, try using these two reminders: "ABC" and "SEE." You first steady yourself with ABC. You change the way you SEE yourself or the situation by changing your lens. Let's spell these all out!

A = Assess your mood

You can't intentionally shift yourself out of an emotionally triggered state if you aren't even aware that you are in that state. You first have to notice that your mood is, or has become, catabolic. This self-awareness sets the stage for all subsequent choices and actions.

As we learned in chapter 7, you need to use the muscle of *self-assess moods, thoughts, and sensations*. With this muscle, you quickly scan yourself for signs of triggers or catabolic energy. If you have already practiced many times before (for example, by using the MindMastery® for Mental Fitness™ app eight times a day), you know what to look for in yourself. You can recognize your habitual patterns. You can quickly determine that yes, your energy is catabolic. Yes, you are triggered. Your brain's amygdala is going wild.

Here's a quick example. You head the customer service department, and there are a flood of complaints from corporate about the way your people are handling problems. Having your team criticized infers that it's your fault. You get back to your desk and you find an email from the CEO. He wants to meet and discuss the issues. You notice your chest is tight and your heart is racing. You recognize the signs: you're triggered. So what to do next?

B = Breathe

The most productive thing you can do next is to calm your nervous system, restoring at least some of your brain's thinking capacity. Breathe to use the muscle of *calming your physiology*. (See chapter 9.) Oxygenate your brain by taking one or more deep breaths and holding each for six seconds. Now your amygdala is beginning to stand down.

C = Choose to take accountability

Now that your nervous system is calmer, you can engage your rational, prefrontal cortex. You can take ownership for your mood and for changing the trajectory of what happens next. You use your muscle to *choose accountability* (chapter 5) for shifting your mood.

That's what the head of customer service did. In the face of complaints from corporate, she said to herself, "I'm triggered." She is aware of what is going on. "Okay, I'm triggered. I'm threatened. Why am I threatened? Because what I'm feeling is that they are saying we are not good enough." That's a core thought that springs from defensiveness.

What she has to do in that moment is identify, "Yes. That's what I feel. But instead of believing I have to defend my department and myself, I need to listen and discover what it is we can do to serve the organization better. To do that, I need to ask questions of the senior staff, such as: Help me understand what we could be doing to improve. What frustrates you most? Are there more issues? Can we sit down and spend half an hour walking through your biggest frustrations with our team?"

When she does that, she's looking at the situation from their perspective, not coming at it from her perspective. She has reframed the situation: This isn't about us failing or not being "good enough." It's about how we can make the organization better.

Making this kind of choice changes the ultimate outcome of your situation because it puts you in charge of driving the train instead of flailing about in the caboose. By making this choice, you understand that you are not powerless. You can take control. And you *must* take control.

Think of an athlete in a challenging game or match. She puts herself into an optimal position to make a play; she is as present and ready as she can be in both body and mind. For you dealing with a triggered state, these actions do something similar. You become aware, you calm your body, and you take ownership for your results. You steady yourself; you ready yourself. You restore your capacity to think and act constructively with your prefrontal cortex. Now you are ready to execute the second part of the shift: you change the way you SEE yourself or the situation, and you do this by working to:

S = Spot your lens
E = Explore other lenses
E = Elect a more helpful lens

With these actions you identify your active lens, explore alternatives, and then elect one that increases the likelihood of a better outcome.

In a way, it is like being at an optometrist's office to get new eyeglasses. The doctor has you look through different lenses as you read a chart of letters on the wall on the other side of the room. Then she asks you, "Which is better? Lens number one or lens number two? Now how about lens number two or number three?" And so on. Ultimately, you choose the lens that works the best for you. It's the same thing here.

S = Spot your lens

The first step is to identify your current lens, the one driven by your underlying operating system. Use your muscle for *self-assessing your thoughts* (chapter 7).

You need to find the dominant thought that's causing your distress. Among the many thoughts you have, which one is at the core of your upset? This thought reflects a perceptual lens that is strongly impeding you. When you find it, you'll usually know it because you'll feel a strong reaction or resonance in your body. At the same time, you may feel a sense of relief because you've gotten to the core of the upset (even though you haven't dealt with it yet).

E = Explore other lenses

Fortunately, your current, active lens is only one of *many* possible lenses. It's just the one that happens to be front and center for you, and it *feels* like the absolute truth. But now, decide to loosen your grip a little. Remind yourself that as true as it may feel, there are always multiple ways to see things. Use your muscle to *engage with multiple perceptual lenses* (chapter 8).

Be curious, flexible, and open. Ideas for other lenses can come from anywhere: your trusted thought partners, books, teachers, God—and from yourself. At first, you will probably draw a blank and need outside input. But by the time you've been doing it for a while, you will have encountered a range of alternate lenses that you can call on in the moment and consider. Because typically there are just a handful of core lenses that cause your triggers over and over, as you find *those* patterns, you'll *also* find a handful of other lenses that are the most helpful to you.

A great way to explore other lenses is to access the multiple "voices" within yourself. Think of having your own inner board of directors. The negative voices are the ones that usually come to the forefront, voices such as "The Critic," "The Judge," "The Denier." But tune your ears past those dominant voices. Encourage the other, more grounded parts of yourself to speak up. Just like a group of real people, the many parts of yourself can offer a wide spectrum of perspectives if you ask them or access them.

You can also leverage your knowledge of people you know. You'll want to pick people who readily hold a distinct lens that you've had some difficulty adopting. This can be a lens of challenge or inspiration; it doesn't matter, as long as it's different and constructive for you. For example, when I think that my natural ideation lens may be going too far, I imagine the critical lens of one of my trusted team members. Conversely, she imagines my possibility lens when she feels constrained by her natural lens of risk aversion. And of course, sometimes we actually talk; it's not all imagined. But the point is, once you know someone, you can ask yourself: What would that person say to me in this situation? How would they look at it? How would they advise me?

E = Elect a helpful lens

Finally, you're ready to change your lens so that you can perform optimally in your situation. Use the muscle to *choose a helpful perceptual lens* (chapter 6). Replace the lens that is holding you back with a different thought that is more empowering or supportive—one that will take you to a higher level of performance. By refocusing in this way, you change what is possible for you to do, be, or experience.

Mindset: Your Most Important Asset

Will you succeed in changing your brain with MindMastery? It depends on your mindset: your set of assumptions, beliefs, feelings, attitudes, and values about what you're planning to do. Your mindset will either *support* your efforts or *sabotage* them.

Your mindset is within your control. If you choose to *believe* that your efforts will be successful, you are setting yourself up for success. If you choose to *assume* there's value in continuing to practice when it's hard, when you're not getting it, when you're struggling—you're creating success.

If you respond to the app only two times one day, but the next day you choose to adjust your *attitude* and recommit to responding to all eight alerts, you're creating success.

Your mindset determines how to come to things, how you relate to them, and how you engage with them. To ensure that you stay the full course with the MindMastery brain-changing process, start by creating your best possible, most supportive mindset that you can.

WALK BEFORE YOU RUN

As a busy leader juggling a very full plate, you may be thinking, "Seriously, who has time for all this practice?" Here's what I say: Can you find just one minute in your day, eight times every day? Not even eight minutes in a row—just one minute at a time, eight times a day? I'm pretty sure you can find eight minutes. Here's what you're going to do in those eight minutes, and why it is absolutely worth your time and attention.

The endgame of all of this learning is to permanently change your brain—to completely rewire your underlying operating system.

Your new, mentally fit, version 2.0 brain will be able to:

- Sustain you in an anabolic state
- Avoid trigger states much of the time
- Rapidly shift itself from the now-rare triggered state back to a neutral or anabolic state
- Consistently perform well under pressure

My approach to changing the brain is direct and efficient. It combines a proven methodology and technology; it's accessible and effective. I have used it with thousands of clients from all walks of life and work. I've seen many dramatic transformations as a result. Key stakeholders, even spouses, have observed transformative shifts in perspectives, conversations, and leadership.

The technology piece is the MindMastery® for Mental Fitness™ mobile app, available on both the Apple and Google Android platforms. You use it to practice applying the muscles of mental fitness as your daily life is happening, and along the way you create real neurological change for yourself. The app supports you through two stages of your development. When you first start, the app helps you build your muscle to self-assess, the A in ABC. This muscle is so critical that we isolate it first as a foundation.

Here's what happens:

- The app sends you an alert eight times at random every day, throughout your waking hours.
- With each alert, you respond by briefly stopping in the moment (or as soon as you can, given that you might be driving or in a meeting).

- You open the app and record your current mood and current thoughts.

That's how you start. One minute, eight random times per day, over a period of several weeks, and you're on your way to changing your brain!

Even in this early stage, you will begin to realize significant improvements and gains. You will begin to catch yourself when you are in a catabolic state. As you become more self-aware, you won't always need the app to prompt you to self-assess; you'll start doing it naturally on your own. Further, you will begin to discover your recurring catabolic thoughts—the thought patterns that create most of your triggered or catabolic moods. That data will be essential later on when you want to quickly spot your perceptual lens—the S in SEE.

How Does the App Affect Your Brain?

The MindMastery for Mental Fitness app prompts you to take actions that *weaken* your overreactive amygdala and *strengthen* your rational prefrontal cortex. The simple act of stopping to identify your mood lowers the amygdala's activation. You're already managing your emotions better.

As you move out of reactivity, you strengthen and activate your prefrontal cortex. Now you have the capacity for more effective conversations and decisions. You stop jumping to quick assumptions and conclusions. You start to play well with others.

The app's random alerts train your brain to *repeatedly* identify your moods and thoughts. This is a new move for you. It signals to your brain, "THIS IS IMPORTANT"—pay attention!" As a result (perhaps after some initial resistance), your brain lends extra energy resources to build your new neuropathways—thus making this easier for you.

All the while, you're rapidly building the fundamental skillsets of awareness, mindfulness, emotional intelligence, and resilience. Because the app *surprises* your brain through random timing, this means your brain *pays attention*—and that accelerates learning.

BUST OUT OF YOUR CATABOLIC STATE

Once you're adept at self-assessment and you are regularly noticing your own catabolic states as they occur, you will be ready for stage two of your development—ramping up your performance. It's time to practice using all of the mental fitness muscles together to shift yourself out of a catabolic state.

Now you will use the app in a different way. This time, you will no longer respond to every app alert. When an alert comes along and you self-assess that your mood is anabolic, then great! You won't do anything with the app; you just continue doing whatever you were doing. However, if you get an alert and you self-assess that your mood is catabolic, then you have some work to do.

You'll open the app and enter your mood and thoughts as you have many times before. But this time, you won't stop there. In that moment, you apply all the mental fitness muscles, going through the full sequence of ABC and SEE. Your goal is to completely shift and reframe yourself out of your triggered or catabolic state—to bust out of it.

If you are a MindMastery client, engaged in our workshops or coaching with one of our MindMastery® Certified Coaches™, you'll have access to some advanced app features to support your practice of busting out. However, if you're not engaged with us, and you're learning this method on your own, you can still do this part of the practice. The important thing is to stop in the moment, and use all the tools you've been learning in this book with the intent to successfully apply them as rapidly as you can. Be a little competitive with yourself: how fast can you do it?

At first, it will take you some time to create that shift. That's fine, and completely normal. As your brain changes, you will be able to shift your mood faster and faster. And you will be making fewer and fewer app entries—and therefore needing to bust out less and less often—because your mood will be catabolic less frequently.

At some point, you will rarely make an entry. Your brain will have changed; you'll shift your own moods rapidly, and without any external prompting. Further, because you have changed your underlying operating system—your perceptual lenses—many of your past triggers won't even occur anymore. Your new brain won't need to go into fight-or-flight. You simply perform.

Exponentially Increase Your Performance

You're busy. You want high performance. And you want it NOW.

Your brain is a biological organ. It has endless capacity to grow and change—but it does this by modifying its own physiology. It actually changes its own internal structures.

When used correctly, MindMastery for Mental Fitness is the most rapid, efficient, and effective way to permanently upgrade your brain. You'll see exponential improvement in your performance—in both leadership and life.

Just take a moment to imagine the benefits of spending most or all of every day in anabolic energy states. You're calmly and effectively performing—almost effortlessly—as you lead yourself and others from your brain's strong, engaged, and rational prefrontal cortex.

POTENTIAL ROAD BUMP #1: YOU WANT A SHORTCUT

You're going to want this whole process—changing the brain, becoming mentally fit—to be done faster. And with less effort. Unfortunately, there are no shortcuts. Your brain has to go through a period of training; both the unlearning and new learning. Making this sustainable change is actually a physiological process. We can't just wave a magic wand.

However, I designed the MindMastery® for Mental Fitness™ app to leverage your brain's natural ways of learning and functioning. This way, we can generate the most change in the shortest time, when the app is used on a consistent, daily basis, eight times a day.

These best practices for brain rewiring include:

1. The element of surprise: that's why the app alerts are at random, not set, intervals
2. Repetition with frequency: eight times a day
3. Duration over time: you will be doing this for some time

Let me explain why these are best practices. Your brain learns faster when it gets a surprise of some kind, rather than sameness or predictability. The technical term for this is "intermittent reinforcement." The app does not allow you to plan, predict, or anticipate when you'll get an alert; the timing is randomized throughout each day, every day. When the alert catches you off guard, that's good! That's what we want. To get your brain's attention, we need to surprise it with an unexpected interruption.

If you find yourself annoyed or irritated by the interruption, take that as a good sign. It means that the app has successfully cut through all the noise around you and has captured your brain's attention. Of course, your brain didn't want that; it was already engaged in doing something else. But that's exactly the point. The app is giving you a tap on the shoulder to say, "Hey, whatever you are doing right now, stop and take one moment to observe yourself."

Your brain also learns faster through frequent repetition. Brain change is a lot like going to the gym. Lifting a few weights here and there won't produce much of a result (not a sustained one, anyway). Rather, you must exercise consistently with both repetition and frequency. Every day, MindMastery® for Mental Fitness™ app gives you eight prompts. That provides you with eight opportunities to repeat the process of overcoming your habitual thought patterns and developing new ones.

Finally, changing your brain requires practice over time. How long? It varies from person to person, determined by your own natural learning curve. But I can identify two things that will get in your way of changing and make the process take longer. The first is that you don't actually get to the core thought of what is going on. When that happens, it is akin to snipping off the head of the dandelion weed but not digging up the roots. When you fail to get the roots, the dandelion keeps coming back.

The second problem is that people don't put in the repetition that's needed. Here's a quick example: A woman had been working with me for about three or four weeks. She had the app but she only made one entry a day. Or one entry every other day. She'd miss a day, and then put in two comments the next day to try to make up. She came to me and said, "Your approach is not working."

I said, "Well, it's like you've been going into the gym for just five minutes at a time, every other day, and you're upset that you're not building any muscle."

I can tell you right now that you and your brain are going to strongly object to these frequent, repetitive interruptions that occur day after day. There will be a natural resistance to change. You will unwittingly slow down or stop the process. You will "forget" to use the app. You'll ignore the prompts. And you will rationalize all of this with thoughts such as:

Eight times a day? Excessive! I'm sure three or four times are enough.

Geez, the app just went off again? I just did this an hour ago! Forget this. I'm not going to write this one down.

It's my day off, I don't have to do this.

I've got this. I don't need to do this stupid thing anymore.

Although neuroplasticity makes it possible for the brain to change itself, doing so takes great effort. Your brain will avoid changing and will tell you it's too difficult, too time consuming, especially at the beginning. This slippery type of avoidance lulls you into doing *nothing*. It tricks you into making no changes. You're very likely to fall into that trap, probably without realizing what is happening. Your brain will be very stealthy about getting you out of using the app, because your brain is driven for efficiency—and ignoring the app means there is one less thing for your brain to do. I guarantee you that it won't always be difficult. And I will guarantee you something else: the return on putting in the work will be well worth it.

While it's possible for you to change your brain, it requires a lot of work primarily because your brain will tell you it's too difficult and too time consuming.

POTENTIAL ROAD BUMP #2: YOU WANT TO AVOID PAIN

You might believe that when you apply this method and develop mental fitness, you will no longer have to feel any emotional pain. No more sadness.

No more fear. No more anxiety or frustration or stress. Mental fitness is your get-out-of-jail-free ticket and you look forward to a pain-free life.

Unfortunately, that is a misunderstanding of what mental fitness is. The intent is not to create some modality where you don't have to feel anything. That's not healthy! The point of mental fitness is to *minimize* pain, not to eradicate it. There is very good reason for some pain, and you do not have to be afraid of feeling it.

When you have *reduced* pain, you can learn to sit with your difficult emotions in a constructive, helpful way. This pain is telling you something really important about yourself, it is sharing vital clues about how you are creating pain in your life. Know this: if you are *creating* pain as a result of your patterns, then you can also "dis-create" that same pain, by *changing* your patterns. You have the power to do this. You don't run away from these feelings or cover them with Pollyanna positivity. You let go of "poor me" thinking.

So, what do you do? You pay attention to the pain. You pause with the pain. You actually allow yourself to experience the deep pain and loss that arise when you repeatedly engage in actions that don't serve. In fact, sitting with pain in this way, in a learning way, is inherent to the development of true mental fitness.

For example, you could be feeling deep financial pain—you don't have enough money to cover the mortgage. Or you could be feeling relationship pain caused by repeatedly impulsive decision-making that has left you in a bad relationship. Maybe you are experiencing the acute pain of being overlooked for promotion—again—because you continue to self-sabotage with emotional reactivity or self-interested agendas. Perhaps you are feeling the intense pain of social isolation because no one wants to be around you, the one who always has to be right.

Your pain is a gift. It actually *is* your get-out-of-jail card—but it's not free. You must allow the pain to reveal those automatic, robotic responses that keep creating those unwanted results. You let the pain guide you toward upgrading yourself. You process it and arrive at deep, new understandings that you then use to change yourself going forward. When that happens, pain becomes your greatest teacher.

Key Points

- **You perform at your best** when you rapidly transform negative moods, or negative physiological states, as soon as they start **by holistically applying all five muscles** of mental fitness.
- That transformation occurs in two steps, requiring you to remember **ABC** and the word **SEE**.

  Assess your mood and notice that you are emotionally triggered.
  Breathe in and hold for six seconds to calm your physiology.
  Choose to take accountability for shifting into a healthier mindset.

  Sense the current lens you are using.
  Explore other lenses.
  Elect a helpful one.

- **Learning how to do all this takes practice.** There is no way around it.
- The payoff is worth it.

EPILOGUE

We've now come to the last few pages of this book, but it's not the end of *your* journey into *leading lightly*.

What happens now?

It matters how you choose to end your experience of this book, how you close it out and put it down. It matters what you choose to do later today, tomorrow, in the coming days and weeks. Because whatever that is (or isn't), you are going to be creating or designing much of what happens from here on out in your work and your life. In fact, you have always *been* creating what's next! But now you are *aware* of that fact.

So, here's what *not* to do. Here's how *not* to end.

Don't fall back asleep. Don't "un-know" the personal insights or "aha's" you've had. Don't push aside—or conveniently "forget"—what you've learned. Don't put your blind spots securely back into position. Don't step heavily back into the patterns of thought, mood, and behavior that no longer serve you.

But it's just so tempting, isn't it? To slip back into old ways—even the uncomfortable, stressful ones. Your brain will find any sneaky way it can to resist change; your underlying operating system will play manipulative tricks to keep itself just the way it is. Remember our forest analogy? How your brain will want to efficiently choose the big, wide path that it knows, instead of whacking through new paths? If you look carefully, you'll see some really enticing road signs pointing you directly down those alluring highways:

SLEEP . . .

FORGET. . .

"THIS NEVER HAPPENED". . .

So, here's what you *can* do.

Make the choice to carry the ideas from this book forward even after you've set it down. Practice and build your mental fitness muscles a little bit every day. Perhaps get some extra support, if that feels right to you.

But in any case, *start where you are*. Ask yourself: What insight or mental fitness muscle made the most impact? How can you build on that? Or, what ideas or skills seemed most accessible, the low-hanging fruit? How can you grasp those pieces and begin to build on them each day?

Now, I don't know when you picked up this book or what your reality is today. As I said in the very beginning, the entire world was in the midst of a global pandemic just as I was finishing up the book. Daily life for most people looked nothing like it had when I began writing just a year before. No one could have foreseen the magnitude of these changes.

Leading Lightly supported me in navigating the challenges to my business, family, and personal life. *Leading Lightly* supported my clients, too. The ones who strengthened their mental fitness muscles and embraced ownership for their experiences were the ones who were resilient, adaptive, and positive. They were the ones who got themselves through their darkest days and provided a steady light for those around them—the people they cared about and those who depended on them for genuine leadership.

Know this: *Leading Lightly* is a way of being. It is the embrace of possibility and the re-creation of the self. It can't eliminate *all* pain from life, but it shifts the balance from ongoing stress and suffering to an abundance of sustainable well-being. Choose it. Choose to lead yourself and others in this way. No matter what is going on around you, *everything will be different.*

APPENDIX

THE JODY MICHAEL ASSOCIATES MENTAL FITNESS INDEX™

In 2018, Jody Michael Associates commissioned a construct and criterion-related validation study of a newly developed mental fitness assessment tool entitled the Jody Michael Associates Mental Fitness Index (JMA-MFI™). Intended for use in coaching C-level executives on aspects of mental fitness, the core idea behind this noncognitive assessment tool is that leaders can learn and apply behavioral techniques that intentionally and rapidly shift themselves out of a fight-or-flight state and into a neutral or positive state of being.

The JMA-MFI tool contained eighty-three items across six subscales that collectively formed an interpretable scale. Part of the validation of the JMA-MFI tool included a comparison of participants' responses to JMA-MFI items to participants' responses to a subset of items from an independent mental fitness tool produced and owned by the HeartMath Institute.

Psychometric and statistical analyses on data collected via the JMA-MFI tool demonstrated that JMA-MFI items form a unidimensional scale (one primary component) that can be expressed in collective terms of six subscales. Extensive item analyses of the JMA-MFI items were conducted. Outcomes identified three items that require review and either editing or contextual clarification. As currently written, form-level reliability of the JMA-MFI tool has a demonstrated coefficient alpha of 0.946 (83 items), which suggests very strong internal consistency among the items and consistency with results from the series of factor and principal component analyses performed on the JMA-MFI items and subscales.

Demographic data were examined and crossed with other measures to explore for any two-way activity or interaction. Other than the proportion of divorced respondents, nothing significant was observed.

A limitation of this study pertains to the general sample of respondents that volunteered to participate. More women than men participated in this study (approximately 2.35 females per 1 male respondent); White was the dominant ethnic group (88.4%). When crossing gender and ethnicity, the majority of participants self-reported as being white and female (N=169; 63%). Unless these numbers generalize to the target population of users of the JMA-MFI tool, then caution should be used if strictly interpreting or applying results from this work.

In conclusion, the JMA-MFI assessment tool yields a reliable, unidimensional scale that is appropriate for its intended uses. Further work should include the setting of performance standards so that certain "scores" have interpretative and clinical value.

For further information or inquiries about the JMA-MFI, please contact Jody Michael Associates (www.jodymichael.com).

MindMastery® Certified Coach™

Are you intrigued about MindMastery coaching?

A MindMastery Certified Coach (MMCC) is a credentialed, professional coach who is approved to use the full MindMastery methodology in their individual coaching practice with clients who have completed the MindMastery workshop.

MMCCs have undergone MindMastery training, supervision, application coaching, and testing through Jody Michael Associates.

If you'd like to experience MindMastery coaching from an MMCC, or if you're a coach who wants to explore becoming an MMCC, please contact us at info@jodymichael.com.

ACKNOWLEDGMENTS

Ever since I was a young child, I wanted to write a book. But time slipped away as I spent years with my head deep in my client work, as well as building and running a thriving business. The book didn't happen. It *couldn't* happen.

At least, that's what I told myself. But to be honest, the real impediment to achieving my coveted goal lay in one simple, recurring thought: *I don't have time.* Ironic, isn't it? Here I am—an executive coach who helps clients reframe their lens to optimize their performance—reflexively repeating my *own* impeding thought!

It took four simple, emphatic words to shake me out of my trance. My good friend Waverly Deutsch, professor at the University of Chicago Booth Business School, cut through all my defenses. "YOU NEED A BOOK!" she declared. To be fair, I'd heard this from others, too. But she was the first person to spark real movement in me. So, to Waverly: Thank you for that impactful conversation, the inception of this book. Thank you, too, for the ongoing support and friendship from both you and your wife, Mary Shea.

As I now think about every other person who has supported me, it is clear there would be no book written, no process created, and no applied research conducted without spending over 25 years and over 40,000 one-on-one coaching sessions with my clients. Thank you to each and every one of you. We co-created this work together!

In fact, I have learned that it takes a village to actually produce a book. I offer my sincerest thanks to everyone who helped bring it to fruition. All of the following companies and people made valuable contributions to this work.

Let me begin with the trifecta that truly brought it all together: My publisher Greenleaf Book Group, my publicist Cave Hendricks Communication, and my social media machine Educated Change. Without this assembled team of talent, the book's reach and impact would not have been the same.

To Greenleaf Book Group: Thanks for believing in my book, my message, and me! Tanya Hall, Jessica Choi, Jen Glynn, Chelsea Richards, Chase Quarterman, Scott James, and Justin Branch: you were all high-level, discerning professionals who made every exchange delightful and productive.

To the Cave Hendricks Communication team: Barbara Hendricks, you exude authenticity, generosity, and passion. I knew the moment I met you that I wanted you and your team to promote my book. Thank you for choosing to work with me. And thank you to Jessica Krakoski and Emily Layelle for your tenacity, teamwork, and spirit to help this book find the right audiences.

To Peter Klein, Samantha Milner, Gabriella Fregona, Megan Poulson, and the team at Educated Change: Thank you for encouraging me to bring my authentic self—the self I bring to my clients—to the world.

Several other people were instrumental in bringing this book to life. Some are core or extended JMA team members, and others are individuals who have played an important role:

To Nancy Scheel: If there is such a thing as a "book midwife" or "book wife," you personified that role. You were with me when I committed to the idea and excitedly dove in. And you were still there much later on when I became weary, unfocused, and exhausted. You were a muse, a friendly antagonist, a coach, a truth-teller, a relentless editor, and a co-sculptor of the book. Throughout our pivots, laughter, and occasional moments of annoyance, you remained a beloved confidante and friend, and a great JMA coach. Thank you. I love you.

To Kelly Brummet: Your gracious manner and outstanding efficiency have never ceased to amaze me. Thank you for handling our day-to-day business—and *me*—while also modeling *leading lightly*. I can't imagine having been on this journey without your presence. Somehow, you managed to keep all the balls in the air with a beautifully light touch. As well, your "closing" suggestions were always on point and poignant. You walk the talk, you are a great ambassador for the brand, and you are a treasured friend and employee. Thank you. And, I know you know this: I love you.

To Kathy Petrauskas in your role as Creative Director: No one knows the ins and outs of my visual aesthetic and brand as intimately as you do. Thank you from the bottom of my heart for contributing your expertise, artistic sensitivity, get-it-done drive, and *time* to bring nuance and beauty to this book—both inside and out.

Many people provided guidance about my early book drafts or helped to polish a final draft for presentation to potential publishers. I extend my deepest thanks to all of you: Paul B. Brown: for helping to shape the book's flow, writing, and structure. Michelle Williams: for finessing and proofing the manuscript. To Cynthia Sherry, Ed Wynn, Doniel Sutton, Suzi Pomerantz, and Wendy Capland: for all of your generous guidance and advice to me as a first-time author. And, I am grateful to Janet Goldstein: you correctly posited that my first book draft wasn't intimate enough, and your creative brainstorming inspired me to create the title *Leading Lightly*. And, to Dale Barr who managed to keep all the threads from unraveling.

As well, I am thankful to Cristina Sotelino and Jacinda Adams, each for your discerning marketing eye.

Finally, to Dana Giambroni: thank you so very much for your humor, your uncensored thoughts, and your critiques throughout.

Alongside the book, a number of individuals made critical contributions to the development of my assessment, the Jody Michael Associates Mental Fitness Index™ (JMA-MFI). I want to acknowledge and thank each of you. To Kirsten Skillrud, for your dedication and guidance with the technical nuts and bolts of building this rigorous assessment. To Joy Mathews (JML), for your technical analysis verifying that the assessment is a valid and reliable assessment for the construct of mental fitness. To Liz Lynch, for your critical eye on the details of the assessment report. And to Judy Mendels-Peterson, for graciously undertaking the admittedly tedious review of the assessment questions.

Leading Lightly is not only the culmination of my professional work; it is also reflective of my personal journey through life. Myriad individuals have indelibly shaped who I am today, and I want to thank all of you. Some of you passed through my life briefly but with significant impact. Others have remained for decades. All of you have had a profound impact on my growth, perspectives, and life. And because of that, the essence of my time with each of you is somehow, somewhere, in this book.

Kathy Petrauskas, my life partner: You are my soulmate. Sharing my life with someone as beautiful, deep, creative, and thoughtful as you, I feel as though I live in a sanctuary. Someone once said to me, "You know you're in the right relationship when it's easy." Thank you for making every day easy—for being my rock, for sharing my aesthetic for beauty, and for the meaning and richness you bring to our relationship.

My parents: In unexpected ways, you were great teachers to me. In experiencing challenges, I discovered the vital need to be deeply intentional in the creation and design of my life. Mom, you taught me unconditional love and the importance of mental fitness. Dad, my childhood environment with you fostered early development of my emotional intelligence. Thank you both.

My beloved Italian family: Your emotional warmth, love, and expressiveness continuously enrich my life. You are the definition of family to me.

Cathy Skopis, my 7th- and 8th-grade teacher: Thank you for your guiding hand and for being there when I needed you as a surrogate mom, lifelong mentor, and friend. You made me feel special.

Judy Mendels-Peterson: Simply put, without you, I wouldn't be who I am today—as a person, as a professional, and as a coach. I love you.

Fernando Flores, my executive coaching teacher and mentor: You shaped my thinking, my work, and my coaching. You and your teachings are alive throughout my coaching philosophy and practice. Thank you for powerfully setting the foundation for the work that I do and love.

Dawn Silver, Doris Hebel, Gary Christian, and Janet Berres: Thank you for your consistently wise counsel and guidance. You've always been there for me.

Eckhart Tolle: I have often turned with gratitude to your teachings, spiritual clarity, and modeling of profound lightness.

Brené Brown: You unabashedly walk your talk; you're authentic, vulnerable, and a great professional role model. Your message deeply connects with me.

To my University of Chicago graduate school professors, especially Mary Jo Barrett, Bill Borden, and Froma Walsh: I deeply appreciate your inspirational teaching as well as your help in cementing my PhD scholarship.

To all the current and past employees, coaches, and extended team members of Jody Michael Associates: Thank you all for being a part of my organization and, by extension, my life. In ways large and small, your skills, talents, and perspectives have significantly contributed to JMA's continuous growth and improvement.

And to the people and close colleagues whose own paths have deeply enriched and intersected my life's journey: Alice Jones, Cathy Cullen, Charles Ifergan, Dore Schreibman, Elise Magers, Joel and Nancy Friedman, Kathyrn Toth, Linda and Gino Agostinelli, Renee Bouck, Susan Fredman and Terri Hawley, Wendy Capland, and Will Stern.

Thank you. I love you all.

ABOUT THE AUTHOR

Author photograph by Robin Subar.

Jody Michael is CEO of Jody Michael Associates, a premier coaching company specializing in executive coaching, career coaching, and leadership development. She is recognized as one of the top 4% of coaches worldwide and is an internationally credentialed Master Certified Coach, Board Certified Coach, University of Chicago trained psychotherapist, and Licensed Clinical Social Worker.

Jody brings a rare combination of global SVP leadership, theoretical knowledge, plus extensive field experience. She's built her expertise through 40,000+ hours of individual sessions across 25+ years of coaching; post-graduate education in human behavior, neuroscience, and psychology; and 15 years in corporate leadership with Goldman Sachs, Chicago Research and Trading (CRT)/NationsBank, and Kidder-Peabody. In her early coach training, she studied for three years with thought leaders Dr. Fernando Flores and Julio Olalla to bring ontological coaching to her leadership positions.

She has been a trailblazer by nature since her youth. Always a visionary, she drove her career development through precise intentions and fearless actions to become one of the first female traders on the Chicago trading floors, a corporate leader in the finance industry, and one of the first coaches in the country. Based on her applied research, Jody pioneered the use of technology in coaching by creating one of the first mobile apps for brain change to accelerate the building of self-awareness, mindfulness, resilience, and emotional intelligence.

Jody has coached some of the nation's top performing leaders and teams across diverse industries and organizations, from hypergrowth tech companies to global Fortune 100 organizations, and has a special affinity for partnering with tech, finance, and healthcare. Among her clients are more than 120 senior executives across 18 Fortune 100 companies.

She's a renowned keynote speaker, author, and thought leader in her field who has been featured in *The Wall Street Journal*, *The New York Times*, *Forbes*, *Oprah Magazine*, *Huffington Post*, *Crain's Chicago*, and more. She has appeared as an expert on MSNBC, CNN, the TODAY show, and NPR.

Jody and her partner, Kathy, reside in Chicago, IL, and Palm Springs, CA. Jody has a deep love of travel, nature, art, and design, and is passionate about curating a collection of beautiful rocks and fossils originating across the world.